"*Growing Up Shared* is a roadmap to giving not only parents, but all of us insights on making educated decisions on what we share online. This book makes a perfect gift for any parent or *expecting* parent in today's digital world."

—Sue Scheff, author of *Shame Nation: The Global Epidemic of Online Hate*

"This thoughtful, nuanced, balanced approach to a complex issue challenges parents to think from the perspective of their kids as they empower them to think and speak for themselves."

—Nancy E. Dowd, author of *Reimagining Equality: A New Deal for Children of Color*

"Every family with an internet connection needs a copy of *Growing Up Shared*. When I start worrying about all the many questions around issues of kids, connection, and privacy, I turn to Stacey Steinberg for practical, real-world advice that doesn't assume a generation of children is doomed because they have access to Snapchat et al.—and that asks us parents to worry about our own online lives as much as we worry about our kids."

—KJ Dell'Antonia, author of *How to Be a Happier Parent: Raising a Family, Having a Life, and Loving (Almost) Every Minute*

"*Growing up Shared* empowers readers to be more empathetic parents and better role models. Read it now and save yourself from significant conflicts down the road."

—Devorah Heitner, author of *Screenwise: Helping Kids Thrive (and Survive) in Their Digital World*

"Finally, an engaging and judgment-free manual to help you figure out that elusive balance between sharing just enough and sharing too much. In *Growing Up Shared*, Stacey Steinberg sorts through this emerging area of concern using both her years of research and her experience as a mom. Grab a cup of coffee, and check in with Steinberg for answers to your digital safety questions. You won't regret it."

—Katie Hurley, LCSW, author of *No More Mean Girls* and *The Happy Kid Handbook*

"*Growing Up Shared* should be required reading for anyone who has ever posted images of their children or grandchildren on social media. Written by an expert on children's law who is also a mother of three young children, the book's goal is to help families develop their own individualized guidelines for safe, constructive, and respectful online communication."

—Barbara Bennett Woodhouse, author of *The Ecology of Childhood: How Our Changing World Threatens Children's Rights*

"Every parent should read *Growing Up Shared*! [The author] presents a balanced look at the pros and cons of sharing our lives online and offers practical ideas for raising social media–savvy kids."

—Phyllis L. Fagell, LCPC, author of *Middle School Matters: The 10 Key Skills Kids Need to Thrive in Middle School and Beyond—and How Parents Can Help*

"*Growing Up Shared* is an incredibly useful resource for anyone raising children in the social media age... This book serves as a useful resource as [parents] seek to protect their children's digital footprints in our increasingly connected world."

—Alexa Fox, assistant professor of marketing at the University of Akron

"Stacey [Steinberg] navigates this complex field, while providing countless examples and approaches so each parent can decide what works best for them (and their family)."

—Andrew Galligan, MD

"Everyone has different comfort levels on what they choose to share online, and...the author...arms the reader with tools on how to share smart and how to better control the narrative."

—Marla Neufeld, assisted reproductive attorney

"Told by an expert from a parent's perspective, this book presents a balanced approach to each topic and gives parents realistic pointers and relatable questions to consider."

—Khanh-Lien R. Banko, member of the Florida Parent Teacher Association (PTA) Board of Directors

# GROWING UP
# SHARED

How Parents Can Share Smarter
on Social Media—and What You
Can Do to Keep Your Family Safe in
a No-Privacy World

# STACEY STEINBERG

Published by Sourcebooks
P.O. Box 4410, Naperville, Illinois 60567-4410
(630) 961-3900
sourcebooks.com

Library of Congress Cataloging-in-Publication Data

Names: Steinberg, Stacey, author.
Title: Growing up shared : how parents can share smarter on social
   media-and what you can do to keep your family safe in a no-privacy world
   / Stacey Steinberg.
Description: Naperville, IL : Sourcebooks, [2020]
Identifiers: LCCN 2019059007 | (trade paperback)
Subjects: LCSH: Internet and children--Safety measures. | Online social
   networks--Safety measures. | Children--Crimes against--Prevention. |
   Internet and children--Risk assessment.
Classification: LCC HQ784.I58 S733 2020 | DDC 004.67/8083--dc23
LC record available at https://lccn.loc.gov/2019059007

Printed and bound in the United States of America.

*To Mason, Isaac, Gabrielle, and Ben.*

# Contents

# Introduction

Our social media networks serve as a parent's modern-day baby book. From posting our children's ultrasound pictures to detailing their accomplishments, our newsfeeds follow their footsteps from cradle to college. Newsfeeds serve not only as a place for us to document these special moments but also as our guide; they're where we turn when we want to ask our friends and family about parenting. Yet alongside the benefits of sharing on social media, there are risks.

I've been an attorney since 2004, a mom since 2006, and a photographer since 2011. Over the years, my roles as memory keeper and memory revealer have been constantly in flux. While sharing my way through motherhood, I began to question whether I was putting my children's privacy in jeopardy and whether their life stories were really mine to tell.

Studying children's privacy on social media fed both my personal conflicts and my professional passions, so six years ago, I delved deep into the work of studying the intersection of a child's right to privacy and a parent's right to share. This research, which began as an attempt to better inform my own decisions, now sits squarely at your fingertips. My goal isn't to make you see the issues in the same way as I do. Instead, my goal is to give you a guide to navigate through the powers and perils that social media offers.

I decided to research this issue to help my own family, and I quickly learned that few scholars were writing on this topic, one that could help parents worldwide. Like many parents, I was sharing on social media without a care in the digital world before I started questioning myself. I went back and forth on my public family blog—one day comfortable sharing the details of my children's colds and the next day feeling fiercely protective of their online identity.

More than once, I deleted posts after second and third thoughts. As both protector and sharer, I sat with the realization that my children had no "opt-out" link, and my split-second decisions had the potential to create indelible digital footprints they couldn't erase. These footprints are a digital trail, a record of sorts, that passively recorded their childhood and may remain visible well into the future. Sometimes I shared on a whim, and I rarely got their OK before posting. And while my privacy settings were set to notify me before *I* was tagged in a post, my children had no control over what I posted (or what I approved others to post) about *them*.

———

There are laws that protect children's information, such as medical, educational, and sometimes even records of online behaviors. These federal laws, called HIPAA (a law aimed at protecting a patient's medical information), FERPA (a law aimed at protecting a student's educational records), and COPPA (a law aimed at protecting a young child's online data), place parents in the driver's seat. Parents decide when third parties—like schools or doctors or sports teams—can share information about their kids. Yet while parents are making these privacy decisions, they are simultaneously posting the very information—potentially sensitive information—they don't want others sharing. By doing so, they are acting as both the gatekeepers and the gate "openers."

When parents post personal information online, they invite a larger community to know details about their child's life. In most circumstances, that might be OK because parent and child interests often align. But that isn't always the case. As the *keepers* of the gate, we are tasked with protecting our children's privacy. But as the gate *openers*, we are deciding when and how to let their stories become part of a larger community.

As law professors Benjamin Shmueli and Ayelet Blecher-Prigat point out in their article "Privacy for Children," sometimes kids have an interest in privacy that is separate and apart from that of their parents.[1] Since I first considered my internal conflict with online sharing, I've gone through periods where I've stopped sharing altogether to periods where I've shared multiple times a day. Before each share, tweet, or post, I've tried to think carefully about its long-term consequences. I haven't always gotten the balance right, and I have occasionally taken down a post shortly after making it. I know I am not alone; parents around the world must also ponder on how to talk about their kids online.

In my quest to better understand how parents can best balance the benefits and risks of online sharing, I met with child advocates, pediatricians, mental health professionals, and cybersecurity experts. They all offered critical insights into the cultural groundswell that has taken place over the past decade. But perhaps more importantly, I spoke to families, specifically the kids who will be most affected by their parent's decision to share.

Throughout my research, I've dealt with two significant questions that shaped my perspective: How has online sharing changed our identities, opportunities, and responsibilities as parents? And how has online sharing changed the landscape facing young people as they come of age?

―――

Over the years, I've concluded that there are no easy answers when it comes to sharing our stories. Being brave and vulnerable—both online and offline—helps us connect with one another. When we open our hearts (and our photo albums) to friends and family, our connections grow. When we share our stories with strangers, we forge new pathways and new connections.

What follows in these chapters is not a judgment of parents who choose to share differently than what is prescribed in this book. As the first generation of parents to raise families in the age of social media, we are forced to do the best we can with the information we have. *Your* information is made up of your family values, including your personal views on privacy and community.

The goal of this book is to give parents tools to make the most well-informed decisions they can before sharing about their kids online. This book also serves as a conversation starter and a guide to help parents and child advocates navigate the many ways social media has changed modern parenting.

This book is also about what others share online about our kids and, for parents, what our kids should share—and not share—about themselves. The information we share creates our kids' digital footprints, and at some point, the personal information they disclose curates these footprints into their online identities. In the pages that follow, I sit side by side with parents who want to do what is best for their kids while staying connected to their friends and larger communities. I turn to the experts—including the parents who live social media, like I do, day in and day out. I use real-life examples and offer real-life solutions for parents and child advocates looking to make sense of this massive experiment we call social media. We are the first generation of parents to have constant access to social media. And our kids are the first generation to grow up shared.

———

I don't suggest we stop sharing about our kids online altogether. Despite all my research, you can still find me—and my family— on Facebook. But I do suggest we stop and think about how our online activity will affect our children in the long term.

Parents don't overshare online because they are malicious; they simply haven't fully considered the significance of their child's digital footprint. If they have weighed the risks and still choose to share, they likely have a good reason for doing so. My greatest hope is that what is contained in the following chapters is not taken as preachy or damning of other parents, who almost always have their children's best interests at heart.

Moving forward, I encourage you to reflect on what you reveal on your social media newsfeed *and* what you hide. This is a book for those who share about their families online every day as well as for those who haven't shared a single picture. Wherever you fall on this spectrum, I encourage you to consider whether there is a better way for us all to connect online while at the same time protect our children's privacy.

What are the benefits to sharing our stories? What are the risks?

## CHAPTER ONE

# Under the Watchful Eyes of Their Parents' Newsfeed

My first son's birth announcement, sent out via snail mail in 2006, was beautiful. I spent hours crafting it on a website in between midnight feedings and early morning diaper changes. The announcements arrived via postal mail, and for many members of our extended family, it was the first they had heard of our son's arrival. Those closest to us—our immediate family and close friends—had some time to get to know him before our larger community knew he existed. Some visited at the hospital. Many even received an email in the days that followed, and of course grandparents, aunts, and uncles all took the time to call. But for many people in our extended social circle, the birth announcement, arriving almost two months after his birth, was the first—and only—photo they had seen. It would be the only photo they would see during his first year, the next arriving with an invitation to his first birthday. I still have a few copies of both the birthday invitation and the announcement tucked away in his baby book, and though I don't open the book often, there's a comfort in knowing it's there.

Our second son was born in 2011. He also has a baby book on his shelf, but his sits almost empty. Most of our second son's milestones were recorded online. I sent birth announcements out via postal mail months after his arrival, but by then, everyone who knew me, everyone who knew my parents, and everyone who knew my husband's parents had already heard the news. Our combined hundreds of "friends" who logged in regularly to their online social networks knew of his arrival within hours of his birth...because moments after he joined us earth side, we had posted a status update announcing his arrival and sharing his picture on Facebook.

While some relatives and friends likely appreciated our connectivity in that exciting moment, not everyone was thrilled by the electronic announcement. It certainly took my dad by surprise. He had driven four hours, late in the night, and sat in the hospital waiting room, down the hall from where my husband and mom held my hand during labor. He anxiously waited for updates, drinking coffee and playing on Facebook. My dad finally got the news he had driven so far to receive, only he didn't get it the way he had planned.

As he scrolled on social media, he learned that his grandson had arrived.

Moments after our son entered our arms, he took his first steps into our Facebook newsfeeds. My dad learned of his grandson's birth not by my excited husband ushering him back from the waiting room but via a tiny screen in the palm of his hands.

———

When I think about our second son's birth story, I used to be a little embarrassed by it, but it mostly made me smile and marvel at technology. The story still makes me laugh, and of course I am grateful that my dad took the whole thing in stride. But now it also fills me with some regret. What did our family lose by not having time to bond with our new son before sharing him with the world? How did our impulse to share make my dad feel as he sat in the waiting room—my mom getting to be by my side during the birth and him resigned to status updates alongside our coworkers and distant friends?

How did this decision to share—and the thousands of decisions that followed in the years after his birth—change life for our kids, whose photos grace far most space on our newsfeeds than they do on our living room walls? I'm an adult, and when I put my own life on display, I'm ultimately responsible for the outcomes. But, my younger kids—well, they didn't get the choice. They had a digital identity long before they were able to speak their own words.

We may question how parenting in the age of social media affects us. We caution ourselves that by constantly posting status updates, we aren't living in the moment. We are warned not to compare ourselves to other parents in our newsfeeds. I'm starting to wonder if we've been focusing too much on the *impact* social media has on our own lives and not enough on how social media *affects* the lives of our children.

How will this sharing affect our children's lives as they grow up with digital footprints not of their own making? I've struggled with this issue firsthand—as a mom, a photographer, and a children's rights attorney. And while I haven't found clear answers,

I've discovered it is crucial that if we are going to spend so much time thinking about what our kids are doing on social media, we need to also spend time thinking about our own choices online. We've had the benefit of crafting our *own* online identities—no one did it for us. But until our kids get older, the ones responsible for crafting *their* online identities are *us*.

## A Generation in Transition

Nothing can ever fully prepare us for parenting, but there are many things we *did* learn from our experiences as children. We watched our parents try to get it right, and we saw fictional parents screw up and succeed on TV. We spent most of our lives with the understanding that one day, we would be parents, and our life experiences would inform the choices we made for our own kids. That gave us time for reflection and time to talk about discipline and dietary choices. Time to consider whether we'd let our babies cry it out and whether it would be best to be strict or lenient with our teens. We even had time to decide how we might react when our kids wanted to play violent video games and when the right time might be to get them their own phone.

We haven't had similar life experiences or time to reflect when it comes to social media. We can't draw true comparisons between our conversations at the lunch table and their conversations over text. Being popular at the homecoming dance looks different than being popular on Instagram. Our kids are the first generation to grow up shared online, and we are the first generation to raise kids alongside social media.[2] This is an area of parenting where we don't get the benefit of our own experiences—neither as children of parents who were online or even simply as observers who watched other parents share online from a distance.[3]

As a mother, I am often guilty of oversharing even the most mundane parenting experiences. My oldest son was born just a year before I created my Facebook account. But even after keeping a baby book for the first two years, his life, along with the lives of my other two children, have since been the highlight reels of my newsfeed, which contain far more milestones than I've written about in their increasingly dust-gathering baby books. My children's images fill my virtual cloud, a place they are only beginning to know exists. But as they enter an age where they can express opinions about their digital footprints, I am thinking about these issues a little more deeply.

Armed with a law degree and a passion for juvenile law, I can't help but wonder if my social media habits will one day be outlined in legal casebooks and social science research under the caption, "Can you imagine?" Once social media comes of age, will we regret all the information we revealed during its early years?

## Legal Rights for Kids

As an attorney, I look for answers in the law, but the law doesn't give us much guidance when it comes to how we use social media as families. While there are laws that protect children's private information online, they protect kids only in the most limited of contexts—and in the United States, parents can almost always share about their children online with unfettered discretion. Most parents try to exercise their discretion wisely. But it is important to stop and ask: Where does the parent's right to control the upbringing of the child end and the child's right—as the person whose information we are splashing on our newsfeed—to some semblance of privacy begin?

HIPAA prohibits medical professionals from sharing personal information about patients without written consent.[4] FERPA requires teachers and administrators to protect the privacy of a student's educational records.[5] Delinquency statutes protect some juvenile records from public disclosure.[6] Societal norms encourage us to use restraint before publicly sharing personal information about our friends and family. But nothing stops parents from sharing their child's stories with the virtual world.

———

When I started studying this issue, I expected to find a legal answer nestled somewhere between the U.S. Constitution and case law. The Constitution sets forth many rights for both parents and kids. For example, it is because of the Constitution that individuals have a right to free speech. There are several additional applicable rights that we have in the United States that aren't in the Constitution but, through statutes and case law, have been adopted by our legal system with almost as much force.

The identified right that I found most relevant to my legal analysis centered on parents' rights to control the upbringing of their children. In their article "The New Law of the Child," Professor Anne Dailey of the University of Connecticut School of Law and Laura Rosenbury, Dean of the University of Florida Levin College of Law, explain that our country used to give almost all of a child's decision-making power to the parents.[7] Over time, U.S. courts started to transfer some control away from parents and to the government. However, parents continued to yield most of the power. As Rosenbury and Dailey explain, "In case after case, the Supreme Court has affirmed the constitutional rights of parents 'to direct the upbringing and education of children under their control.'"[8] Parents want laws to help our kids thrive in the age of social media, but when it comes to child-rearing, our country has given parents a lot of deference with regard to how they raise their kids.

————

Despite this reality, many parents are beginning to recognize that there is a conflict inherent in a parent sharing about kids online. In the United States, children are not guaranteed a right to privacy, especially one that is *separate and apart from* her parents. While kids may have rights to privacy in other contexts, they *don't* have a right to privacy *from* their parents, except in the most limited of circumstances. Courts are reluctant to grant children privacy rights in the context of family life.[9] Even when a court recognizes a child's reasonable expectation of privacy, the court often places higher value on the interests of the parent, family, and the state in exercising control over the minor child. The legal system does not offer us guidance when it comes to balancing a child's right to privacy with a parent's right to share.[10]

Unlike the United States, most other countries guarantee a child the right to privacy through an international agreement called the United Nations Convention on the Rights of the Child (UNCRC). The UNCRC "is the most complete statement of children's rights ever produced and is the most widely-ratified international human rights treaty in history."[11] A total of 195 countries (every UN member state except for the United States) have ratified the treaty.[12] Article 16 grants children this right to privacy, and it is often referenced by the international community. In a publication written by UNICEF's United Kingdom Partner, the right to privacy means that "the law should protect the child's private, family and home life, including protecting children from unlawful attacks that harm their reputation."[13] The United States signed the UNCRC, but it is the only UN member country not to have ratified it, which means it is not law or formal policy here.

## Why Parents Share

Shortly after becoming a mom of two, I fell in love with photography. I love capturing the moment, and I adore sharing my work. Years ago, I would have needed a gallery exhibit to show off my photos. But when I purchased my first professional camera in 2012, all I needed was an internet connection. My photography quickly took on a life of its own. By the end of 2012, not only was I photographing my own family, but also friends and strangers were hiring me to photograph theirs. I started a small photography business, promoting my work through Facebook. In 2013, I established the Shared Hope Project, offering free pictures to families who had children with chronic illnesses. With each family's permission, I shared these amazing and brave stories online.

I'd always been a social justice advocate. All of a sudden, my camera and my computer offered a way to make a difference, one click at a time. Through my photography, I saw the benefits of sharing online firsthand. The stories were featured on social media and in many news outlets including the *Huffington Post* and the *Washington Post*. These human experiences raise awareness for important social issues and help secure funding for important medical research. When struggling families share, others similarly situated gain support and knowledge. As a result, we all can deeply connect with one another and recognize the rich diversity in society.

———

I also saw the benefits of social media as a mother and close friend to other families who benefited by allowing themselves to be vulnerable online. For example, my friend Heather has struggled with sharing about her son's complex medical disorder.[14] On one hand, she appreciates the need to protect his digital footprint, and she has some concerns about oversharing his medical information on social media. On the other hand, she knows that by sharing, she is helping families on her newsfeed become more aware of the need for additional funding to support research. Sharing their experience connected Heather to other families dealing with the same issue. It helped her locate additional medical resources to support her son, which have been life-altering.

Just like her son's condition, Heather's decision to share was complex. And like so many other parenting decisions we make, she did the best she could with the information she had. In the end, that information led Heather to being comfortable sharing parts of her son's story online. They are both better for it.

I, too, have tried to balance the competing interests of online sharing. Like most parents, I want to put my children's needs above my own, or at least act in a way that aligns our interests. This is hard for me. Sometime between the birth of Facebook and now, I started thinking about myself as the protector of my children's digital identity. I am still learning how to balance this role with my desire to share my own story.

Unlike parents of the future, I don't have a lot of research or data to guide my decisions. This is the parenting issue of our generation, and the conversation is just beginning.

My kids had online footprints long before they stumbled upon egg surprise videos on YouTube. Their likes and dislikes, medical concerns, and silly quotes graced my Facebook feed before they started unlocking my iPhone. My journey through motherhood is documented in public blog posts and sappy op-eds, many of which I now regret. By broadening my lens and looking at "sharenting" (defined by *Collins Dictionary* as "the habitual use of social media to share news, images, etc. of one's children") not only as a mom, but also as a children's rights scholar, I've changed how I share. I've started to think a little deeper about the information I post online about my kids—I've started asking if their pictures are really mine to share.

## Sharenting = Online Sharing about Kids

From what I can tell, the term "sharenting" was first used in a *Wall Street Journal* article two years before I ever started researching children's privacy.[15] It even was added to the approved list of Scrabble words in 2019.[16] But more than just being a popular word, it is a word that is used to describe the *action* of a parent sharing on social media about parenting. There are examples of over-sharing, which is probably not so good, but there are also examples of sharenting that most parents would find perfectly appropriate. The word tends to be polarizing—some think it's a fine descriptive word, but others hate it. My hope is that this book will *not* be polarizing. My goal is to *inform* parents—not to pass judgment on *any* parent.

———

A Pew Research Center study found that more than 60 percent of parents reported receiving helpful parenting information online within the past thirty days.[17] In this same period, half benefited from the social support and advice they received on social media. Almost a third of parents have asked a parenting question online. These parents overwhelmingly turn to social media for more than just staying in touch with old friends. Over 75 percent of parents who use Facebook log on every day, and more than half do so multiple times a day.[18]

One friend, Lisa, says that she sees online sharing as a way to connect to and support each other. In many ways, it helps people feel like they are a part of their friends' lives. But even though Lisa sees benefits, she thinks that the *way* people share isn't always a good idea. Once you put something out there, it can be hard to take back. Lisa worries that if she posts information about her kids, eventually they'll see it, wish it weren't there, and they may not be able to remove it. As we curate our children's lives on Facebook, we create their indelible digital footprints. Our initial decision to post information may have consequences that won't easily be forgotten.

Our online interactions give us the benefit of having a support group available at any time. Some parents participate in support groups focused on specific issues—children with hyperactivity disorders, parents seeking healthier lifestyles, breastfeeding support groups, and countless others. For parents who engage in these groups, the information received can be life-changing. The groups may offer new and better ways to interact with their children, and other members can offer support during the many challenging moments of parenting. Parents have access to more information than ever before. But in order to participate in this vast network, parents often must disclose details about themselves and their children.

## How Do You Share?

Consider the following true/false statements. You can write out your answers in the space below or make a mental note.

When I share online, I am concerned that I am intruding on my child's digital identity.

True | False

Sharing online makes me feel brave.

True | False

Sharing online makes me feel vulnerable.

True | False

I hope to advocate for my family's values when I share online.

True | False

I hope that by sharing online, I can better build my own social network.

True | False

I hope that by sharing online, I can stay in touch with family and friends.

True | False

I don't like to share any personal information on social media.

True | False

I don't like to share personal information with large groups of people online, but I do like to share with smaller groups on social media.

True | False

I never share online because I feel like there are too many privacy risks.

True | False

I never share online because I do not have a social media account.

True | False

When I see others sharing about their kids online, I can't help but judge them for oversharing.

True | False

My child deserves to have "veto power" over what I post online.

True | False

My child is too young to have a vote in what I post online.

True | False

I want to model good online citizenship for my children.

True | False

I want to stay present in my offline life as much as possible.

True | False

When I share online, I look forward to seeing friend and family reactions.

True | False

Come back and revisit your answers when you get to the end of this book. Do your online actions align with your values? If not, how can you get them in sync?

CHAPTER TWO:

# How Parents Share

Over the past decade, I've gone between immersing myself in social media one day and completely removing myself from it the next. I've been excited by the interconnectedness the internet offers but also fearful that all this sharing violates my children's privacy. I know I am not alone. My friend Cara told me that when she first became a parent thirteen years ago, "every breastfeeding question and every minor illness had me calling the pediatrician's office. I always knew I had friends and family that I could reach out to, but few were dealing with kids the same age as mine, and I often needed advice at odd hours of the day." Cara told me that as her son got older, she struggled to help him behaviorally, and at the time, she didn't realize how common her parenting issues were. This caused Cara to feel alone in her struggles.

"When my oldest was seven, we added a second kiddo to the family, and wow—what a different experience it has been! From the time my first child was born to the time I welcomed my second, parenting changed—our support moved online," Cara explained. "I'm a member of two online parenting groups for mothers, one local and one with members across the globe, whose participants have kids within one month of my daughter's age. Anytime I have a question, I can post it to the group, and I'll have ten answers within the hour. I'm starting to think about the digital footprints I've inadvertently created for my kids. Sure, I made the choice to share, but I am not so sure I've fully thought it through."

Deborah Lupton is a professor at the University of New South Wales in Australia, and her research focuses on digital sociology. In her article "It Just Gives Me a Bit of Peace of Mind," Lupton explored why mothers in Australia often turn to social media.[19] For the most part, the women found their online experiences to be positive. These mothers often shared very private and intimate details of their lives with other moms via online parenting groups. Having this space to talk about things like sex during pregnancy and their feelings as new moms gave these mothers a feeling of support.

While they did not know the other mothers personally, these mothers felt safe sharing information in their virtual life that they might not have felt safe sharing in other spaces in their brick-and-mortar life. As part of her study, Lupton interviewed almost forty women using three focus groups. Some of the mothers indicated that while they initially got to know the other moms via social media, they often met or planned to one day meet in person.

## Styles of Sharing

Many scholars around the globe have made similar findings. In "Sharenting = Good Parenting?"[20] Maja Sonne Damkjær spoke with young Danish parents about their experiences sharing online. She analyzed their social media posts and identified the following four social media communication styles that defined how these parents shared.

1. **Family-focused social media user.** Damkjær's research revealed that many Danish parents, like their American counterparts, use social media to keep family updated on their children's growth and development. These families shared ultrasound pictures, family events, and other childhood milestones. The posts were geared toward nurturing existing extended family relationships. While family and friends commented on the posts, the feedback was usually short and, like many of my own Facebook newsfeed posts, rarely led to deep online conversations. Most of the parents on my social media newsfeed use the same style of sharing.

One mother I spoke with, Joy, believes her sharing falls into this category. Joy is a hardworking mom of two. She is a community organizer and tries to create meaningful relationships both online and offline. Joy shares on social media in many ways. There was a time when she shared more in smaller, interest-focused groups because, as a preeclampsia survivor and mom to a preemie, she felt her "normal" looked very different from that of other moms on her newsfeed. "So many of the people I knew with full-term babies left me feeling panicked over things that my child couldn't do," she said. During that time, she became close with other moms who had similar experiences, other moms who were also trying to adjust milestone charts to account for their children's early birth.

As her child grows, Joy's need to find similarly situated moms has waned. "My posts these days are focused on sharing with family and close friends, but also keeping a digital baby book for my family. Not as concretely as some moms who might even print them, but more of a record and reminder to myself for the future. Those little conversations and developments that I wouldn't remember to record otherwise make it to my newsfeed, and then years later, I am reminded and can compare them to how things ultimately played out."

While Joy enjoys sharing online, she is aware that many people on her feed are professional contacts or people who don't know her kids. "I tend to use the kids' initials more than their names. The people who know us know their names, and the ones who don't, don't need to. I also don't have my last name on my account, and I try very hard to only friend people who I have actually met rather than friends of friends."

2.  **Peer group–focused social media user.** Damkjær noted that some parents in her study mostly shared through private or semiprivate Facebook communities. She explains that an important part of this communication style involves the parents "participat[ing] in one or several large (mostly closed or secret) due-date and parenting groups on Facebook anchored and initiated online." This reminds me of many of the parenting groups I've joined over the years. I've traversed in and out of these groups at various ages and stages in my kids' lives, sometimes to learn about a struggle my kids were experiencing or to bond with parents whose kids have similar interests as my kids. Unlike family-focused sharing, the comments on posts in these groups were often much more extensive, with peers offering feedback, advice, and support.

My friend Tonia, a high school teacher and single mom of one adorable little guy, uses social media as a support group. "I understand that there are drawbacks, but in my opinion, it does me more good than harm because if I am better and have less anxiety, my child also benefits." Tonia has connected with other moms though social media since her son was a baby. "When I was pregnant, Facebook was more basic; I didn't see anything even remotely like that. We were the beginning of those sort of mom support groups." Her son was born in 2012, just as parenting support groups were taking off. "The more I shared, the more other parents were willing to share. The group got me through a lot of sleepless nights. I was communicating with other moms who were sitting in rocking chairs doing exactly what I was doing. I realize the gravity of that. It was really powerful."

Now that her son is getting older, the questions have changed, but the group dynamic really hasn't. "We no longer ask those 'new mom' questions. We are talking about school, our kids' education, and sometimes their behaviors. The regularity of the posts has slowed, but there are still posts daily." I asked Tonia if her status as a single mom affected the frequency of her posts or her overall usage of the group. "I think it had little to do with me being a single mom, but more to do with my personality. My child is my world. When I share, I like to share about him."

Tonia recognized there could be risks to sharing personal information, and she was eager to learn more about what I, as a privacy researcher, would look out for. As I prepared to respond, I thought of the many times I wanted to share in an online group, and how torn I've been weighing the benefits of getting feedback from parents against the drawbacks of sharing with people I don't personally know. While we may join these groups believing that the other members have shared interests and experiences, we may inappropriately rely on this bond, risking oversharing private information with an audience who may not have our best interests at heart. Information shared within peer groups can be shared across multiple platforms (for example, a user could take a screenshot) without the permission of the original poster.

3. **Oppositional social media user.** Unlike parents who use the first two communication styles discussed, oppositional parents rarely share personal information about their children. These parents use social media but often express their distaste for sharenting. For example, Damkjær explains, "[These parents] worry that their son eventually might feel embarrassed about sharenting posts, and they think that children should shape their own digital identity when they come of age." These parents have strong negative views about sharenting, and they share these views with other social media users.

My friend Naomi is an oppositional sharer. A mother of two, Naomi feels strongly that her children's life stories are not hers to tell. "I can talk about motherhood from my own perspective," she explained, "but it is important that the lens is focused on my side of the story, not theirs." Naomi analogizes sharing a child's story to what would happen if someone shared something about another adult without their permission. She feels strongly that there are private moments we all have—children and adults alike—and that it is a violation to share those stories on social media without getting permission from the other person. "I can't really ask my kids for permission—they are too young and don't really know what 'public' means," Naomi explained.

Naomi does not share *any* photos of her kids on social media, and she gets upset when other parents share images of their own children. "I wish I didn't have such a strong reaction," she admitted, "but I get concerned." Naomi gets frustrated when she sees parents share pictures of their kids doing personal things, like sleeping or reading. These are their private moments, and she worries that by sharing these pictures, kids could get a false sense of what safety and privacy are. "These kids may grow up thinking it is never possible to have their own private space," she told me. "That shouldn't be normal." It's not just concerns about privacy that stop Naomi from sharing online. She also thinks it makes offline interactions awkward. Some of her friends share a lot, and when they see each other after a long time apart, she's not exactly sure what to do with all the information she's gathered from their newsfeed. "Am I supposed to pretend I don't know every detail of their life? I don't want to sound like a stalker, but the truth is, I've seen a million pictures—asking, 'What have you been up to?' seems pretty forced and fake."

While some people use social media to stay connected to friends and family, Naomi finds it doesn't help her feel close to the people she cares about. "I'm not really sure that as humans, we are supposed to know *that much* about each other *all* the time," she explained. "Maybe some of that sharing is really anxiety-based," Naomi opined. "It seems like some people share so that they don't lose touch with people. But I strive to have more intimate connections with my friends and family. I am going to gain more from one weekend together *in person* with my friends than a whole year of being virtually connected on social media."

4. **Social Media Non-User.** Most of these parents choose not to use social media at all, even to share about their own lives. While they may share pictures of their children with more private audiences, they avoid social media almost entirely.

Some of my friends who choose to avoid social media do so because they recognize the intangible harm that can come with living our lives online. They know how quickly it can take them away from their present experiences. In my experience, these parents have conviction that stories are better told face-to-face (or text-to-text), and they value not only sharing their family's experiences, but also hearing back directly from the person with whom they shared. To a large extent, social media takes away that intimacy, and these friends are unwilling to sacrifice it for whatever perceived benefits online sharing might offer.

Jacob hasn't used social media since Myspace in 2003. Now a dad to a beautiful first-grader, he doesn't have any social media accounts, nor does his wife. Jacob's primary reason for avoiding social media is the longevity of information once it is shared online. "When you post stuff, you are posting for life. Opinions change. Preferences change. The entire world changes. Why put yourself out there like that?" he explained. Second, he recognizes that while there are people in his past he likes to stay connected to, he can do that without social media. "The people from my past that I want to see and talk to are the people I pick up the phone and call. I make plans to visit. I don't need Facebook to do that."

Jacob's decision to stay off social media has little to do with being a dad or even privacy. He just really doesn't care for social media and doesn't think having it would add any value to his life. Jacob's choice hasn't affected his family life at all. His daughter is a competitive horseback rider, and Jacob frequently visits the barn's Facebook page for updates. "You don't need a Facebook account to view business pages," he told me. Jacob has no desire to be in a parenting group, so he doesn't miss the Facebook group features. Jacob acknowledged that he might not see as many pictures of cousins and friends, but that doesn't concern him much. "If someone wants me to see a picture, they can text it to me. If I want to share a picture, I can text it to them."

Unlike most parents I spoke with, Jacob is not on the fence about much of anything. He was steadfast in his decision to avoid social media long before becoming a parent, and he has not wavered on his decision.

———

I also spoke with Lea, a mom who has one young daughter. Lea loves to plan special outings with friends and family. She knows how to make any holiday Pinterest-perfect. Lea takes lots of pictures, but she does a great job staying in the moment, perhaps partially because she isn't worried about sharing the highlight reels. You won't find Lea sharing her beautiful memories by posting photos on Facebook, because she's made the choice to stay off social media entirely. "I don't need social media to tell me that I have a wonderful life and a beautiful daughter," she explained. "I don't need that validation from anyone outside of myself." She also knows there are downsides to sharing. At work, Lea sees how social media can cause problems. "I see the harm of social media firsthand," she says. Lea works for a large company and often handles complex issues that require online investigations and research. The digital trail left on social media can be very revealing.

But most important to her decision is her interest in protecting her family's privacy. "I want my daughter to make decisions for herself independent of what I think or what I do." As an example, Lea shared that as a young adult, she wrote an article that is still available online. While she has no issue with the article's content, the digital footprint has long outlasted its welcome. "But, unlike decisions a parent might make for a child," Lea points out, "that decision was mine. I wouldn't want my daughter to grow up and say, 'My mom made a mistake when she shared that information about me.'"

Despite her family's decision not to share, Lea knows that her daughter might choose a different path one day. "I am already having conversations with her. She wants her own YouTube channel." Lea's daughter is young, and instead of just shutting her down when she asks, Lea talks about her decision not to share. "We don't believe in that as a family," Lea tells her daughter. "As you grow up, we can reevaluate it—as a family." Lea wants to have deep discussions as a family about social media and privacy. "I value her voice, and I want her to make her own decisions when the time is right."

During our conversation we bonded over the many things we have in common despite our differing approaches to social media. Lea loves the internet. Like me, she too has to remind herself to stay off her phone sometimes. "At the end of the day, I just don't want social media in my personal life," Lea concluded. "I've decided that I want to protect my child's digital footprint so that when

she grows up, she can be whoever she wants to be without information I've put out there getting in the way."

———

While Damkjær outlines these four communication styles, her
work is careful to not pass judgment on which style is best. As
culture shifts take place, she acknowledges that there are societal expectations surrounding what parents should share and how
much information we should be revealing. Damkjær writes, "The
majority of parents in this case study reported that they were met
with requests to share their new family life on Facebook, especially pictures of their child." The parents she interviewed weren't
only sharing because they wanted to share. Many were sharing
because they felt a societal obligation to participate in our new
online culture.

## Why We Share

One friend, Amanda, explained to me that her life overlaps with
her kids', so it's hard to draw the line between protecting their privacy versus restricting her social connections. She has some simple
rules she always follows: never post anything embarrassing, never
post anything overly personal, and ask, *Will this be important to me
a year from now?*

Sometimes we share because we feel some sense of obligation to show friends and family that we, too, have exciting lives.
While some parents are fine with the unabashed showcasing that
takes place daily on social media, others find it overwhelming and
anxiety-producing. Forbes columnist Carrie Kerpen explained,

"Whether it's on social media or in life, it's easy to start comparing ourselves to others, especially when we are feeling particularly vulnerable."[21] Discussing this issue in a Forbes.com article, Kerpen quotes pastor Steven Furtick as saying, "The reason we struggle with insecurity is because we compare our behind-the-scenes with everyone else's highlight reels."

When I spoke with Naomi (the friend I mentioned earlier in this chapter), I told her that in some ways, I was envious of my friends who are able to resist the temptation of sharing accomplishments online. While she doesn't post anything, she said she understands the temptation. Naomi encouraged me to ask myself, *Who will be genuinely happy to see this?* Naomi sees that many parents share because they are bursting with pride. "Share the news with someone else who will also burst with pride!" Naomi recommends. "That isn't everyone," Naomi reminded me. We joked that these people are usually our mothers, who, like us, find every picture we take breaking news-worthy.

Naomi runs a successful website and blog, and works hard to maintain connections with her followers, who are often her real-life friends. Sometimes, when she is scrolling her newsfeed, she feels like she has to "like" every post, as if it's the responsibility of a good friend to respond. We can avoid these traps by reframing the questions we ask ourselves before sharing. Instead of posting because it makes us happy, Naomi suggests we "post with purpose," even if that purpose is only to make other people smile. "When friends go on a trip, I don't need to see every single unedited picture. I don't need to know every detail of their flight delay," Naomi half-joked. "I don't need a post every day with a million pictures, or the post with, 'Sorry I forgot to post yesterday, we were so busy!' If you were too busy to post, what makes you think I'm not too busy to look through your tenth slideshow?!" Naomi said this not trying to be cold but making the point that our social media highlight reels have now taken the place of the old-fashioned vacation slideshows we used to make family sit through at holiday gatherings. "Please, just don't," she said with a smile.

———

I took an informal poll of parents in one of my social media groups to better understand why parents shared personal information online. Here are some of their thoughtful responses.

**Question: If you've ever shared something personal on social media, were you able to help yourself, your family, or someone else by doing so?**

- Just within the week I've shared very personal things—like a weird rash on my nipple or my struggle with pregnancy-related depression. But the nipple thing was in a breastfeeding group and the depression was in a pregnancy group. In both cases I got helpful feedback. It doesn't feel inappropriate to me because of the venues. I wouldn't have posted a picture of my rashy boob to my Facebook page for all my friends and family to see, but it's not considered weird or TMI in a breastfeeding group.

- No pictures, but I shared words in a group. I was able to get the help needed.

- Yes, I have posted on social media asking for medical advice (i.e., references for local specialists, tips on how to help my child sleep better, etc.).

- It helped me feel more normal about what was going on.

- Yes, but that oversharing tends to be in more private groups on social media rather than a general post to my profile. I also have my profile account pretty secure. I'm very much aware that my parents and my boss are my "friends" on Facebook, so anything I post is going to be seen by them.

- I can't say I do this a lot, but sometimes knowing you're not the only one struggling with something helps.[22]

———

We have a definition for sharenting. But what exactly is over-sharenting? Professor Anna Brosch explores this topic in her article "When the Child Is Born into the Internet: Sharenting as a Growing Trend among Parents on Facebook."[23] She notes that while we might share for help and community, we also share for self-realization and maybe even for social approval. While parenting can often be an isolating experience, social networking makes us feel less alone and more connected.

Brosch explains that "problems arise when parents share pictures of moments that might embarrass their child now and in the future... Apart from present security risks and the permanence of online content, it may cause other consequences in the future. Due to sharenting, children grow up with an entirely different concept of privacy. Thus, it might seem to be normal to them that everything is in the public domain. In this way, the idea of privacy is quickly disappearing."

## Blogging

Professors Alicia Blum-Ross and Sonia Livingstone are two of the leading scholars in the field of digital privacy rights for children. In their article "Sharenting: Parent Blogging and the Boundaries of the Digital Self,"[24] the pair reflects on the common practice of blogging about parenthood. They start with one of the questions that has gnawed at me since beginning my research. They ask, "Where does the parental self end and the child's self begin online?" The pair asks whose story is being shared, and to whom the information belongs. "Related tensions arise regarding privacy in the digital age: is sharing a child's image publicly a violation of that child's privacy? What if the parent's purpose is to reveal and reflect on their own parenting? Who should decide when to share a family photo?"

As part of their research, the professors interviewed seventeen parent bloggers. The authors explained that many of the bloggers were writing to have a record of their family members. They didn't do it only for family and friends, but more for themselves, as something they could look back on one day. For some parents, this was an extension of the work they already did for their kids. We are the sandwich makers. The allowance givers. The memory keepers.

Blum-Ross and Livingstone capture the conflict at the heart

of sharing our stories by exploring what they call "overlapping 'spheres of obligation' that shape everyday decisions about what, where and how much to share."[25] They suggest that this includes our responsibilities to ourselves as parents and our responsibilities to our children—both what they may need now and what they may need years into the future. Recognizing that there is more to telling our stories than our own benefits, the authors note that sharing can also benefit the larger community, a topic I explore deeper in the next chapter.

Importantly, Blum-Ross and Livingstone don't conclude by telling parents whether blogging is right or wrong. Instead, they recognize that we are all new to social media, and that we are all trying our best to find a way to cultivate our online identities to better serve us offline as well. This isn't easy to do academically; we are facing "shifting sands," the authors explain. Finding a way to balance these conflicting interests is challenging both as academics and as parents.

## Avoiding the Overshare Trap

One mother, Renee, told me that she shares online often, and she is starting to think that maybe she should be more mindful about it. Her daughter is a gymnast, and she knows she probably should think about the negatives before oversharing her daughter's accomplishments. Renee shares because she has many close friends and family members out of town, and social media is a great way to keep them involved in her family life. "I always show my daughter the comments that people post. Just knowing that friends and family can see the pictures right after something happens is cool.

Most definitely, I think social media is a good thing, but I can see the downside. It's not just good-intentioned people online. There are some crazy people out there, too."

———

I asked parents in my parenting Facebook group to give me examples of oversharing. Here were some of their responses.

**Question: Do you think some parents share too much on social media? If you answer yes, can you give an example?**

- A Facebook friend recently showed her young daughter sitting on the toilet, potty training, and I believe this was too much.

- Personal conversations they had with their child or things they thought were "funny" that their kid said.

- Yes! I think sharing embarrassing stories or discipline issues about your kids (especially tweens and teens) seems really inappropriate and can get back to them.

- Yes, I have some friends that have their profiles set to public. They post things like bath time pictures or pictures of the kids at their games (while they also "check in"). This gives strangers too much information regarding your children.

- I think it's too much to share every moment of the day or private moments with children or spouses.

- Some parents reveal the exact address of their home or personal things about an older-age child who might one day resent that information being on the internet.

- Sharing intimate details about discipline or "teachable moments" like potty training. Things that could be embarrassing later in life for the child. Relationship issues. I'm not saying social media should be all unicorns and rainbows...but there are some things I don't need to be able to read about your family, IMO.

- Children's illnesses or preteen girls nearing their "time of the month" is not something that should be public knowledge!

- For example, it makes me feel uncomfortable when parents post photos of their children crying or having a negative behavior that is meant to be funny but is really shaming their child. Someday that child is going to see that, and that makes me sad.

- Mainly when the kids get older and you can visibly tell that they aren't happy about their parents sharing things.

- Sharing embarrassing or naked photos of their children.

- I hate when people share about more personal, possibly embarrassing, moments like potty training. I get how difficult it is, but your kid might find that one day, or worse, some bully finds it and makes fun of your child.

- Sharing every single thing their child says or does. It comes off as bragging.

- Yes! I think shameful posts—"Look, my kid is so stupid. They won't do their homework, make fun of them with me," or making fun of anger or sadness, "Look at how angry my child is, I'd rather share on the internet than connect with my kid"—is really heart-wrenching. I expect those posts to negatively impact the future of those parent-child relationships.

- Sometimes parents and grandparents get annoying about it. I particularly felt this way when I was struggling with infertility—I had to "defriend" some people who just constantly posted nothing but baby pics. Of course, I feel the same way about people who constantly post updates about their workout routines.

- I've seen oversharing, but everything is at that family's discretion, and I don't see the need for mom-shaming over it.

- I think some parents share about kid/teen misadventures/ behaviors, etc....and that not all of that should be made available to others.

- I think knowing your child's school, age, and classroom information is too much.

- A friend showed me her granddaughter and her friends in bikinis (they are twelve or thirteen) on a public post on Instagram. That just seemed like too much. That type of post should at least be locked down.

- I think it is oversharing if they are posting information that would compromise safety.

- I've seen parents share too much, but I respect each parent's decision as they make it for their family.

- I don't need to see twenty photos of your kid a day or know every time they reach a milestone.

- If they have their profile public and they post when and where they are at places—it's like, "Hey, look at my cute kid. We are at this park. Come snatch her!"

- I think photos showing any "bathing suit" areas are inappropriate, as are mental health diagnoses without the express approval of the child, some medical conditions depending on how likely they are to lead to bullying or future employment/insurance discrimination. There is a line regarding romance ("So-and-so has a boy/girlfriend" is fine, but "I caught them having sex last night" is not).

————

So where is the balance? A study by the University of Michigan[26] found that the parents who benefit from social media are the same

ones who also see friends overshare. "Sharing photos and anec-
dotes helps distant relatives and friends stay in touch. Connecting
with another parent who is awake in the middle of the night can
help to counteract feelings of isolation. Asking for other parents'
recommendations can facilitate the choice of a new childcare provider. Hearing about strategies used by other parents can offer
practical tips to deal with a toddler's behavior problem," wrote the
researchers.

But like the parents I spoke to, the researchers also highlighted
the downsides of sharing too much and the complexities of deciding where positive sharing ends and oversharing begins. "Parents
also recognize that there can be downsides to sharing too much
information about children on social media. For example, over-
sharenting may occur when details shared on social media are too
personal or are potentially embarrassing to the child when he or
she is older. Although there are no hard and fast rules about what
is appropriate to share, this poll found that three-fourths of parents think another parent has shared too much information about
their child online." Other concerns about social media use pertain to fears that postings could be used to identify a child's home,
childcare, or play locations. In certain situations, such as child cus-
tody disputes or domestic violence cases, disclosure of identifying
information could pose a significant risk.


## Telling Our Stories

When I am not lawyering or teaching, I'm parenting, and all too
often I'm doing so with a camera in hand. Recently, my son was
recognized at Hebrew school and received his first official prayer

book, complete with his name and an inspirational inscription written into the front page. I immediately photographed him, and I asked him to let me photograph him a few more times as we walked to the car.

As we got home and settled into our Sunday routine, I took out the laptop and started to edit my pictures, something I love to do. I then shared three of my favorites on Facebook. My son was cool with it. He was proud of his accomplishment. But as I shared, I also wondered—did I share because I was proud of his accomplishment, or was I proud of the way I captured it through the camera lens?

Naomi, my friend from earlier in this chapter who never posts photographs of her children, shares universal parenting stories through her art. While her Facebook page is not a blog in the traditional sense, her drawings are shared widely on various social media platforms.

"Even though I never share anything private about my children online, I still really like to share. Motherhood is a story worth telling," Naomi explained. A professional illustrator, Naomi will take a photograph and draw the scene from her perspective. She recognizes she is lucky to have the skills to do this, and she acknowledges that without an art form, this is really hard to do without violating a child's privacy. When Naomi shares, her goal isn't to share *her child's* experience, but *the universal* experience of motherhood. A lot of the time, Naomi puts herself in the drawing—in a way, she does this to protect the child, "almost like a parent holding a child's hand as he crosses the street." Earlier in the chapter, I highlighted how Naomi tries to "post with purpose," and she does this through her art. Her goal is to share about *herself and her child,* and also to share in a way that makes *everyone see themselves* in the art. "I use a personal experience to find an element of parenthood that applies to all of us."

## Data-Driven Decision-Making

There is no shortage of advice for parents trying to help their teens use social media safely. However, parents don't have much guidance to help them know how to use social media in a safe way that helps, not harms, their children's online identities. Society educates young people about the risks oversharing poses to their personal lives and future job prospects. We want to educate them so that they don't jeopardize their future. For these young people, the decisions they make online—much like the decisions they make in the real world—are *their* decisions. We can only exert a finite amount of control over their online disclosures. However, as parents, we have full control over what *we* share about them online. Isn't it ironic that so much attention is aimed at their online behavior and so little is focused on ours?

———

Turning back to Lupton's focus groups, a handful of women were concerned that the information they shared on social media and through parenting apps could pose a danger to their families. In one of the focus groups, the conversation turned to the potential risks of sharing online. "It was evident from other discussions that women had with each other that they were aware of the commercial nature of some of the websites and apps that they used. For example, several women in different groups made references to the advertising that they received on Facebook or Google Search changing since they had begun to search for pregnancy-related topics or buy pregnancy products online. This had made them [realize] the extent to which these platforms were able to monitor their online interactions," she writes.

Certainly, the Australian mothers Lupton interviewed felt they profoundly benefited from their use of social media and parenting apps. However, her study also noted that the social media sites and the apps also benefited by receiving the information shared willingly by these mothers. Lupton writes, "Like other forms of caring consumption, these practices are inextricably intertwined with the capitalist ethos of purchasing good and services. However, they are not only about the consumption by pregnant women or mothers of commodities. The digital data assemblages that are configured on pregnant women, mothers, their foetus and children have themselves become valuable commodities that can be exploited by other actors and agencies for profit. The more that women can be encouraged to use apps and other digital media and to contribute details of themselves and their children as part of using these media, the more potentially valuable data they generate."

## Key Takeaway: Parents Struggle to Find a Balance

I get it. I feel very much like the parents in Lupton's study. I love the instant feedback I get when I share pictures, and I value the advice gleaned in parenting Facebook groups. Perhaps more frequently than some of these parents, I've held back from sharing out of concern that these forums present some moral, and perhaps safety, concerns for my family. However, in most ways, I sit side by side with the parents in these studies, and side by side with the millions of other parents wanting to tell their story while simultaneously protecting their children on social media.

I spoke to my friend Tonia about Lupton's focus groups, and she acknowledged that she, too, had similar concerns. However, she pointed out that when she shares, even with a smaller audience, she's thought through the post. "I share information that I am comfortable sharing broadly." Tonia isn't ashamed or embarrassed about the information she's shared. "I always ask myself, *Am I sharing too much? Am I comfortable with my child seeing this when he is older?* If I can say yes, then I press share."

Like me, Tonia has retracted and deleted posts right after posting because she had second thoughts. "My gut instinct kicks in sometimes, I guess, that makes me think maybe it wasn't an appropriate thing to share." For example, she's posted about some of the struggles of being a co-parent and quickly realized she didn't want her son to one day stumble upon the post. "It is rare, but it has happened." She also realized someone who knows her son's dad could see it. "I really do try to ask myself, *Five years from now, will I be happy I posted it? Or will I regret it?* If I don't have a good gut feeling, then I don't post it. Because I just don't know, and I'd rather err on the side of caution."

While the culture shift began taking place about a decade ago, parents are only now beginning to think about how our connectivity has transformed our parenting culture. Children's lives have been saved through the connectivity that social media offers parents, for example by helping parents find doctors who can provide life-changing medical care. Friends who have children with special needs have connected with other parents who are similarly situated, their lives enriched by these powerful new relationships. We've witnessed society transform as we've learned about faraway families facing tragedy from natural and human-made disasters, and we've been touched to offer our support as they improve their lives. We've received support as we've navigated through a new food allergy or a night with a feverish baby. And we've shared daily joys with family members living around the globe, tweeting and sharing as our families grow.

## CHAPTER THREE

# The Power of Narratives

It was 6:30 a.m., and the sun was starting to peek out over the horizon. I took another gulp of my coffee, pulled up to the valet at the hospital, and began to gather my belongings. I checked my camera to be sure I had a formatted memory card and fresh batteries in my flash.

As I grabbed my bag from the back seat, I couldn't help but notice the mismatched socks, leftover granola wrappers, and wrinkled school flyers that littered my car. I took a deep breath, thankful that my kids' seats were empty. I was not at the hospital for them that morning. I was there for four-year-old Phoebe.

About six years ago, I started taking pictures of sick children. I look for smiles in hospital rooms and look past IV poles in hopes of capturing the fleeting moments of carefree childhoods that exist alongside tragic diagnoses and crippling test results. I look for little hands grasping onto hospital beds as toddlers take their first steps in brightly decorated triage rooms. My heart skips a beat when I see an older sister smile at a younger sibling, knowing that siblings, too, suffer when their loved ones are sick. The families almost always share the images on their personal social media accounts and on pages and websites they've set up to support their children.

In the age of social media, it is easy to run across pictures and stories of kids facing devastating odds and feel helpless. As I stood by Phoebe's bedside that day, I felt that way too. Phoebe had been recently diagnosed with DIPG, an aggressive brain tumor. While there were treatments available to improve her quality of life, the long-term prognosis for all kids with this diagnosis is tragically grim. It was for this reason that her parents wanted to share Phoebe's story, in hopes that one day there would be a cure for kids like Phoebe.

During the twenty-nine months that Phoebe survived after her devastating diagnosis, I photographed Phoebe and her family over a dozen times. I got to know Phoebe through my photography visits. I took her pictures, but we also told each other knock-knock jokes and played with her dog, Maggie.

In 2018, Phoebe passed away. In her short time earthside, Phoebe touched my life deeply. She made me a better mom, a better friend...a better person. I loved being able to give something to her family—I couldn't help their daughter get better, but I could give them the gift of memories.

## How Screens Connect Us

A few months after meeting Phoebe, I was asked to talk about my experiences working with chronically ill children and their families. And while I am a former litigator-turned-law professor, I struggled to find my voice. It wasn't until the very end of the talk, when the parents of these children addressed the audience, that I finally heard the words I was hoping to say. Phoebe's dad, Cole Dooley, a physician and brain tumor awareness advocate, stood up and addressed the crowd. "Please don't feel sorry for me," he pleaded. "Get angry. Get involved. Demand better funding for childhood cancer research."

Social media gives communities the opportunity to get involved. It gives us all a chance to get angry.

I had connected with Phoebe in person; meanwhile, she had thousands of connections on Facebook. Through the family's Facebook group, Phoebe's Friends, these connections grew over the course of Phoebe's life. Phoebe's family shared short updates about her adventures and sometimes shared the pictures I took. With each post, Phoebe was able to touch more and more lives— just as she had touched mine.[27]

———

Social media offers us the space to express, the network to connect, and the power to greatly impact our world. When the popular Facebook group Humans of New York shared stories from a renowned pediatric cancer doctor, donations rolled in to support his work, raising millions of dollars for pediatric cancer research. When families started pouring ice water on their heads as part of the "ALS Ice Bucket Challenge," families all over the globe learned about amyotrophic lateral sclerosis, also known as Lou Gehrig's disease. And when same-sex couples across the country fought in the court system for marriage equality, many took to social media to share their own personal narrative, shifting societal discourse on a crucial social justice issue.

## Connected Parents, Stronger Families

Families can harness the power of social media to connect with others, to get help when they are struggling, to raise awareness for medical issues—including mental health—affecting their children, and to change the narrative when advocating for social change. In order to do this, parents must be vulnerable, and often they must make tough choices about what, and how much, information to share about their children.

*Vulnerability.* It is a powerful word. Social media helps us amplify our vulnerability. It allows us to share our struggles, to bear witness to one another's pain. But it also creates a place where real change happens, not only because our voices are loud, but because our voice—our vulnerability—is authentic.

I've often been struck by the power of my friends' narratives. Scrolling my newsfeed might be a time to see cute baby pictures and cat videos, but in between the pictures and videos, I often read narratives—heartfelt stories of friends overcoming mental illness, family members battling debilitating chronic conditions, coworkers being discriminated against on the basis of race or gender. It is this activism that often gives rise to larger, cohesive groups of individuals who band together to make life a bit better for themselves and for people who haven't yet found their voice.

Many of the parents I spoke with share their more intimate stories not on their newsfeed, but in Facebook groups. "I go through phases of sharing entirely too many photos of my children on social media," one mother told me. "Being a stay-at-home mom, I feel lonely and disconnected. I feel like my kids are the only thing I have to talk about, so I talk about them."

Another mom explained, "I think people [overshare] for support, which is OK if that is what they need."

## How We Benefit

In their article "Connected Motherhood: Social Support for Moms and Moms-to-Be on Facebook," Bree Holtz, Andrew Smock, and David Reyes-Gastelum researched why parents choose to engage on social networking sites.[28] They found that parents benefited from Facebook groups for several reasons. The researchers explain that "social support sites may also allow users to feel more empowered. The information shared by individuals can help others make more informed decisions and empower them to take different actions than they may have previously considered."

Holtz, Smock, and Reyes-Gastelum surveyed anonymous users of an open Facebook group called Ask the Chicks. This Facebook group was a little different than many I'd been a part of. Instead of group members posting questions and commentary with their name attached to the post, in this group, every post was anonymous. Group members would send their questions to the administrator, who would post the question on the user's behalf. Individuals could then respond to the administrator's post. Almost 650 group members participated in the researchers' survey.

The researchers reported that many of the parents responding to the survey found the group generally positive, enhancing their social media and parenting experiences. In the comment section, some participants reported that they would participate more often but were hesitant to do so because the group was an open group, and they were worried other friends viewing their newsfeed could potentially see it. The researchers concluded that groups like Ask the Chicks were helpful for a number of reasons. First, individuals didn't need to have an account or give their name when sharing. Second, the researchers reported that the group offered social support, and generally this can "reduce levels of stress, which can improve overall health and quality of life." The researchers also noted that since social media users are often on Facebook, they could benefit from the frequency of their participation.

There are downsides to all Facebook groups, even ones like Ask the Chicks. Managing a group that requires administrator approval for every post takes a lot of work. I can also imagine many ways that a group like this could give members a false sense of security and anonymity. But despite these drawbacks, the success of this particular Facebook group suggests that social media users *want* to share online. By thinking creatively, maybe we can find safer ways to tell our stories.

―――

During my research, I became fascinated not only with what families share, but also with how researchers collect and analyze data. Some of the findings support my theory that narratives are powerful—not only to help change society, but perhaps also to help *see* societal changes that are on the horizon. We know that social media activity can certainly affect public policy. In my article "#Advocacy: Social Media Activism's Power to Transform Law,"[29] I explored how social media advocacy has revolutionized social justice movements. The evidence that social media significantly impacts public policy is resoundingly clear. For example, MIT scholar Amy Zhang and Microsoft researcher Scott Counts found that by examining state residents' past social media posts, they could "predict with approximately 80% accuracy whether a potential policy change will pass given features taken from prior social media posts within the state, and that this method performs better than using polling data."[30] This research lends itself to the theory that, indeed, social media *does* have a substantial effect on the law.

## Who Else Benefits?

Most of the studies I found significant in my social media advocacy research were completed by scholars, but one intriguing study didn't come from folks in an ivory tower; it came from Microsoft. Munmun De Choudhury, Scott Counts, and Eric Horvitz co-wrote an article called "Predicting Postpartum Changes in Emotion and Behavior via Social Media."[31] Their article studied patterns in postpartum women's Twitter posts to try to predict which women would be more likely to have postpartum depression. The goal of the study was to "use social media to identify mothers at risk of postpartum depression, an underreported health concern among large populations, and to inform the design of low-cost, privacy-sensitive early-warning systems and intervention programs aimed at promoting wellness postpartum."

The study reports high levels of accuracy with its prediction capabilities. By studying the social media posts of new mothers, the study authors were able to predict with a 71 to 80 percent accuracy rate which mothers would have "extreme changes postpartum." That is a startling figure, and it is interesting to imagine how this information might be able to help women in the first few months as a new mom, but it also raises privacy and ethical dilemmas.

As I delved into the research, I wondered how I would feel knowing that my social media posts were being analyzed by apps to predict how I might behave in the future. The study authors highlight that "this type of research, and also results on the kinds of inferences that can be made from publicly available data, pose interesting questions for individuals and for society more broadly." The authors fully acknowledge that some women might not want this curated information shared, but they point out that these predictions are similar to predictions systems make about people online all the time.[32] They use the example of how a website might recommend a book to a shopper based on books that shopper purchased in the past.

That said, the researchers also recognized that there is something different about the kind of information being collected in this particular study. They write, "People may be uncomfortable with the possibility that third parties might have the ability to predict future psychological states, especially when relatively accurate predictions can be made about future illness and disability. We believe it is important to bring the possibilities to the fore, so as to leverage the benefits of these methods and ideas to enhance the quality of life for people, as well as to stimulate discussion and awareness of potential concerns that need to be addressed at the individual and societal levels."

If the purpose of this type of study is to create some sort of early warning system, it would naturally need to be shared to be effective. Would women want their posts analyzed like this? What about the 20 to 29 percent of women who just liked to vent online but showed no sign of postpartum depression offline?

## The Cumulative Effect of Sharing

My house backs up to a retention area. The rain can fill the area in a few short hours during a summer storm. When we get a big rain, it looks like I live on a lake.

But most of the time, the area is dry. It makes a great spot for my kids to play ball, and I often take photography clients through it for family sessions.

Every now and then, when we head out there to play catch, our feet sink down into the saturated mud. It takes us by surprise—the ground looks sturdy, but then I remember that it had rained a bit that week.

The power of our voices on social media can be a bit like the rain. Sometimes voices are loud—they overtake our newsfeeds. Change happens in those instances like the big rainstorms—seemingly overnight.

But sometimes, our voices are quieter. When we share our stories, change might look more like the raindrops. One colleague on your newsfeed admits she had postpartum depression. *Drip.* Another shares a GoFundMe page for a baby whose mother took her own life. *Drip.* A close friend with a new baby at home acknowledges she is suffering. *Drip.* A cousin shares a link to legislation to require insurance companies to cover mental health screenings for new mothers. *Drip. Drip. Drip.*

Before we know it, our newsfeeds reach saturation. Like the field behind my house, I can't ignore the fact that it's been raining. My eyes have been opened, my consciousness stirred. If the kids want to play in the field, they'll need their rain boots. If my friend has a baby, I might now be more likely to keep an eye out for the warning signs of postpartum depression.

———

When is it OK to be vulnerable online? Should we always wear our heart on our proverbial sleeve?

What is a sleeve anyway when it comes to our newsfeeds?

There isn't a one-size-fits-all answer to that question, and I am not proposing that we all embrace full vulnerability online. As the next chapter will explain, there are many risks to sharing our stories, and like the cumulative effect of the raindrops, they aren't always apparent. With each disclosure, we offer more personal information not only to our friends, but also to companies and possibly those who wish to harm us.

We might not all be better off for sharing more, but we are all better off for listening to those we care about, and we could use our new knowledge to better our families, our communities, and ourselves.

## Tools for Effective #Advocacy

Historically, social movements have used a number of avenues to enact change, but perhaps the most visible and most effective is the political process.[33] This usually involves groups of people mobilizing, and the work often involves lawyers or policy-makers. These leaders use narratives to effectuate social change.[34] Community-building also offers an avenue for social movements to change the status quo. Instead of seeking change through impact litigation and legislative advocacy, social movements have worked within existing systems, encouraging community leaders to see things in new and different ways. This sort of team-building eliminates the "us versus them" mentality that can exist when a social movement is pursuing change through legal action. While many social movements hope to change the law, informally mediating with community influencers can often create inroads to change perspectives on key social issues.

Social media has transformed how narratives are used to change minds and policies. Sometimes families share online with the purpose of changing hearts and minds, but other times, the advocacy is incidental.

———

Perhaps most relevant to the advocacy discussion centered in this chapter is the role of social media on "incidental advocacy."[35] Incidental advocacy reminds me of my raindrop example. We have an opportunity to educate, to inspire, and to normalize life experiences across diverse audiences.

Scholars at the University of Michigan looked at the role of social media in the lives of LGBT families.[36] Social media offered the parents a powerful advocacy tool. Sharing on social media allowed the parents to "assess social cues from within their personal networks, which helped participants determine how much and with whom they could share." After initial posts, these parents were able to selectively share with supportive audiences. Social media also afforded parents opportunities to find "fellow travelers." These parents benefited from connecting with parents who had similar life experiences.

The University of Michigan study reported that "LGBT parents, however, are especially mindful of their children's right to privacy, both [now] and in the future. Parents in our study worried their personal social media posts might unintentional-ly reveal sexual orientation or gender identity information that could later affect the privacy, safety, or comfort of their children and families."

———

Before deciding to be an online social justice warrior, it's prudent for families to think through the benefits and potential costs of sharing their family's personal narratives with their virtual family and friends. Compelling commentary can quickly go viral, which may seem optimal at first glance but could have lasting unexpect-ed consequences down the road. While you may want to be a social justice warrior, does your child feel the same way?

Last year, my son was bullied at school for being Jewish. My husband and I were devastated. We spoke to the school, we shared our sadness with our Rabbi, and we vented via text to friends. We even reached out to the Anti-Defamation League, hoping to get some guidance in the face of a situation that at first glance seemed to have an easy solution (punishment of the perpetrator) but turned out to be an epidemic without a clear cure-all. There had been multiple anti-Semitic incidents at school, with multi-ple perpetrators. And to make things even more complicated, our son wanted no part in any sort of restorative justice work by the offending students or the school.

Meanwhile, my husband and I have decent-size social media followings. We had both spoken out against anti-Semitism on our newsfeeds in the past, and our instinct was to do the same this time. However, we wanted to balance our son's request to not "make a big deal of it" with our own want (and feeling of responsibility) to shed light on the issue. We were really at a crossroads. How could we balance our desire to use the incident as a larger advocacy opportunity with our son's desire to simply forget about it?

## Creating a Framework for Discussion

Like with most aspects of family life, there isn't one universal solution. We decided to talk to our son about why we wanted to share, we listened to him explain why he wanted to stay out of it, and we compromised on some guiding principles we both could agree to.

▶  The three of us were not ashamed of the incident and were OK with people knowing it happened.

▶  The three of us wanted the offending students to face punishment and learn from the experience.

▶  The three of us were proud to be Jewish and were happy to share this part of ourselves with the public.

▶  The three of us wanted to share with others about the Holocaust survivors in our family, and we all believed it was important to share our Holocaust survivor heritage with the public.

▶  We also disagreed about a few points.

▶  My husband and I didn't mind talking about the rise in

anti-Semitism, and we were fine with people asking us about why anti-Semitism is so hurtful.

▶ My son did not want to talk about anti-Semitism, did not want to talk about what happened, and did not want to explain why anti-Semitism is so hurtful.

By identifying these areas where we agreed (and disagreed), we structured a social media post that met my husband's and my interests (to share and raise awareness) with my son's interest (to not have people talking to him about the incident or about anti-Semitism in general). The post garnered a lot of attention, and it led to some great conversations. My son was interested in the comments and feedback. It was authentic #advocacy.

## Balancing Risks with Benefits

There is so much power in sharing our stories. But before sharing personal information, no matter how influential it may be, take a step back to consider the long-term ramifications of doing so.

Some parents post about their children's mental health, and others post detailed information regarding their children's medical conditions. There clearly are benefits to sharing these experiences. By sharing, families with medically fragile children can connect with one another. These families break down stereotypes, help raise money for important research and advocacy, and often receive support from the community. But some adults with chronic disabilities have expressed concern about these sharing practices.

Despite the risks for many parents of disabled children, parents act as the child's "only voice."[37] If society did not support these online disclosures, the realities of raising children with disabilities would often remain hidden. These family stories help create the patchwork of community that our society depends on for important research, advocacy, and support.[38] Mary Farmer, a mother who has blogged about family life since 2012, made a great point that her choice to share, as a mom of a special needs child, was no different than any other mother's choice. It all came from a place of doing what a caring parent would do in order to best support her child. Their sharing, just like ours, comes from a place of love. Few parents set off to share maliciously; we do it to improve our lives, our children's lives, and the lives of others in our communities.

## Amplifying Our Voices

There is no doubt that the power of social media can and should be harnessed to effect change in our homes, our communities, and our world. The good that sharing on social media can offer often outweighs the harms caused by adding to our family's public profile. If we choose to completely shy away from advocating online for things that matter to our families, we miss critical pathways to change in society. We take away the human element from important policy debates, we remove the face from the names of debilitating diseases, we remove humanity from the stories in our history books.

We can amplify our voices by sharing but in a way that honors our children's individuality and privacy wishes. As we think through these issues, we can invite our children to join in the discussion.

———

I'm the grandchild of Holocaust survivors. My son is the great-grandson of refugees. The history of our people, the Jewish people, is ingrained in our blood. Most of the time, the stories we've heard from past generations play out in our minds as reminders to support others who are being oppressed, as we've luckily led a privileged life in the United States in so many ways. When my son faced anti-Semitism at school, I tried to balance my instinct to share with his hesitance to speak out.

Over the next few months, the bullying got more intense, and my son decided he wanted to share his experience with a larger audience. He was hesitant, but he was upset and knew something had to change. Together, we started small, publishing something in our tight-knit community through a private Facebook group. The response was incredible. He quickly had friends and acquaintances reaching out and offering their empathy and support. With his OK, some of these adult friends started a petition, asking the school board to take anti-Semitism more seriously and to help protect kids targeted by bullying. The petition was shared on social media, and my son asked to share the petition himself on his Instagram feed, where it remains today.

I could tell he was moved by the public support he received. Jews and non-Jews signed the petition, and in less than two days, it garnered more than one thousand signatures. As we prepared to go to the school board meeting to present our concerns, my son decided that he, too, wanted to speak out. He didn't need my voice—he had found his own.

"I wasn't thinking about [sharing] tonight," my son told the school board, in front of a packed audience. "Then we had the petition...and because of that, I thought it would a good idea to share this," he started as he shared his story and told of specific instances of anti-Semitism and bullying. "When I go to school, I don't feel too safe. I think that by sharing...about my story, about other people's stories, I can help people understand what it actually feels like to be called those things," my son said as he finished his speech. "Schools shouldn't be a place of hate."

## Key Takeaway for Advocating Online as a Family

Social media may be the cause of many ills in society. But used effectively, it can also be the solution to many of its problems. By sharing our stories while being aware of the risks of oversharing, we can reach each other's hearts and minds in ways that never before were possible.

## CHAPTER FOUR

# Online Risks

It becomes almost routine: Snap a picture of the kids, crop and edit it, share it on Facebook. Repeat.

Posting pictures of kids on social media has become a fixture of modern parenting. Helicopter parents, free-range parents, even soon-to-be parents are sharing everything online. While our connected culture makes it easier to stay close to friends and family, it also makes it easier for data thieves and predators to take advantage of our well-intentioned efforts to nurture our relationships and grow our social networks.

We must ask: Is it just our friends applauding our kids' efforts in the crusade to end gun violence, or are nameless people sitting at faraway computers creating profiles of our social justice warriors?

If you share regularly, take a quick break from reading and visit your social media newsfeed. Wait—set a timer first. I know how quickly we can get distracted by the never-ending scroll of the social media abyss. What was the first picture you ever posted? Are you able to quickly find it? What other long-forgotten pictures did you find along the way?

It's likely that your social media habits have evolved over the years, and even if you still share a lot, I'd venture to guess you share differently than you did when you first joined social media. For one, you've become more comfortable online, and you've figured out how to curate your life more wisely over the past decade. You might also notice how few "likes" your pictures got in 2007 compared to now. This isn't because you take better pictures now (although the cameras on our phones have certainly improved). It's because social media's popularity has grown, and so have your friend lists.

Just as *your* digital fluency has improved, so have the third parties who are waiting for the opportunity to take advantage of your online disclosures. It's one thing when these third parties act in a way that could harm *your* digital identity, but your protective instincts are probably on high alert if you think someone could be targeting *your children.*

## Digital Identities

We know there are a plethora of reasons that businesses, governments, and nefarious individuals want our digital information. "The most obvious of these [risks] is the growing demand for and use of big data and the rapid development of technologies for its collection and analysis," UNICEF researchers Gabrielle Berman and Kelly Albright highlight in their article "Children and the Data Cycle: Rights and Ethics in a Big Data World." "More data will be collected on children over their lifetime than ever before. The result is that the future use, applications, and consequent impacts on their lives, is still largely unpredictable."[39]

I remember the day I got my first BlackBerry device. It seemed so cool. I could get emails. I could take pictures. I still needed to do most of my work from my computer, but it was an incredible addition to my work-life balance.

It was also a nice addition to my parenting repertoire. My oldest son was two, and I had already been blogging about his life for about a year (something I now regret). We were at the mall, and I took a picture of him on an escalator, eating an ice cream cone in his stroller. I knew I'd want to share the picture on the blog, but for the first time since blogging, I didn't have to wait until I got home. I was able to post the picture instantly, right from my BlackBerry at the mall. *Wow!* I wrote. *I was able to post this from my phone! How cool is that!* I marveled at the technology.

Sure, ten years later, I think it's the exception to post from a computer, and it's far more common for us to share on blogs and social media directly from our phones. But that isn't really my point. My point is that what once seemed impossible is now routine.

## Big Data

In May 2019, I was contacted by Allen St. John at Consumer Reports regarding one of the more recent children's privacy concerns—one that concerned Amazon's Echo Dot Kids Edition.[40] A complaint had been filed to the FTC (Federal Trade Commission) by a number of privacy groups. The complaint asserted that even after parents requested that the information shared by their children on the device be deleted, the information remained on Amazon's servers.[41] According to the Associated

Press, the complaint filed to the FTC alleged that "Amazon is violating the federal Children's Online Privacy Protection Act, known as COPPA, by holding onto a child's personal information longer than is reasonably necessary."

As of this writing, Amazon denies this claim; however, it is one of many issues that parents need to consider when bringing technology into their homes and, through that decision, giving companies access into their children's private lives. The allegations contained in the complaint are extensive and include such concerns as indicating that many of the third-party apps kids use on the Amazon device do not have privacy policies, that the device holds onto information after parents request deletion of the data, and perhaps most importantly, that the guidance Amazon provides to parents is unclear, specifically that Amazon does "not adequately notify parents of their right to control their children's information."

———

When it comes to big data, it is tempting to think only about the risks, but we must consider the benefits as well. Some of these benefits are uniquely helpful in the context of kids and teens sharing. Researchers Berman and Albright highlight some of these benefits "relating to their protection, their safety and their participation within the broader global community."

Berman and Albright explain that law enforcement uses online tools to collect information that is indicative of child abuse. "Technologies developed by Microsoft and Dartmouth College are used to 'tag' child abuse images both online and in cloud-based storage, thereby allowing law enforcement and other agencies to rapidly identify and detect any reproduction of these images," the authors explain. To that end, the FBI has tools that can help identify illegal images being uploaded to the dark web (which is defined by dictionary.com as "the portion of the internet that is intentionally hidden from search engines, uses masked IP addresses, and is accessible only with a special web browser: part of the deep web"[42]). This is especially helpful for protecting children online, and it illustrates one of the benefits of big data in the privacy context.

## Image Theft

A few years ago, while I was first delving into my children's privacy research, I came across an image of a naked toddler on Facebook. The child was positioned so that the viewer could see her bottom and her smiling face, but her frontal private area was hidden from the image's view. The toddler's picture had been turned into a meme that had gone viral. The toddler was chubby, and the photo was captioned, "When you overdid it for the holidays." A lot of my friends thought it was cute, but I was appalled. How did this child's naked body end up shared by so many of my friends? Did this child's parent know that the picture had been made into a meme? How would the child feel if she saw this image when she grew up?

The possibility of the child running into the image on her own was real. I did a reverse image lookup on Google. (Yes, that is a thing. You can insert an image into Google's search bar and see where on the internet the image has appeared.)[43] The image had been shared thousands of times.

It is also possible that the parents had no idea their child's image had been made into a meme. If they shared the picture with a limited audience—online or even through texts, someone could have downloaded it and reused the image. Most people wouldn't do this with a picture of a child they had a personal relationship with, but it's easier to repurpose an image of a child we've never met and use it in a way that may seem harmless but could cause damage to that child if he or she ever actually ran across it. It's unfortunate, but online, people seem to get careless. The person in the picture is dehumanized, perhaps. Consider all the memes you've seen of kids you've never met. Consider the times you've laughed at the memes. It's OK. I've regretfully done it too. Kids are cute. And unfortunately, it's easy to forget that those are real-life kids who likely did not consent to "going viral." Those are real-life kids who may one day grow up to resent their online stardom. Those are real-life kids whose parents might not have even been the ones who turned them into stars.

———

Even parents who share only a few pictures online can find themselves in a vicious situation where someone is using the pictures for bad purposes. Are these people taking note of how old our kids are, and will they pay attention to our child's favorite places to visit? While child abductions and stalking are rare occurrences, the risk is heightened when personal information is shared, giving potential offenders detailed information about a child's life, his or her physical location, and the family's routine.

For example, when one mother, Paris, posted a picture of her child on Facebook,[44] she received a "like" from a user whose name she did not recognize. "The stranger had made the toddler's image her homepage photo and was presenting Paris's son as *her* own child."

Paris is not alone. Another mother, Ashley, experienced a similar form of digital kidnapping. After posting a picture of her two daughters, Ashley found that it was shared by another Facebook page that seemed to share many pictures of little girls. As Ashley looked closer at the link of her children, she realized that any of the thousands of followers could link back to her own Facebook page and track down more information about her daughters, including where they lived. And even more recently, a mother found that an individual had stolen a photo she had posted of her child on Instagram. It showed her young son wearing his wrestling uniform. The thief shared the image on his page, which had many followers who appeared inappropriately interested in young boys.[45] "A spokesperson for Instagram told *Today* Parents that they removed the account 'for violating our policies, specifically using our products with the intention of sexualizing minors.'"

## Digital Dossiers

If the risk of people stealing an image isn't scary enough, parents also need to consider the risk of data thieves stealing a child's personally identifiable information (PII). By tracing a parent's social media data to voter registration materials, children's identity can be inferred, including name, location, age, birthday, and religion. The full gamut of ways this can be used against kids is not yet known. What we do know is that this gives strangers access to information most parents would want to keep private, and it also opens the door for data brokers to steal and trade a child's information in dark ways.

One study suggests that 92 percent of two-year-olds already have an online presence, and that one-third appeared on social media sites as infants.[46] Another study by Tehila Minkus, Kelvin Liu, and Keith Ross, who at the time were researchers affiliated with NYU, suggests that when children appear in Facebook photos, 45.2 percent of the posts also mention the child's first name, and 6.2 percent reference the child's date of birth, allowing viewers to establish the exact age of the child.[47] On Instagram, 63 percent of parents reference their child's first name in at least one photo in their stream, 27 percent of parents reference their child's date of birth, and 19 percent share both pieces of information.

According to the NYU researchers, "Data brokers build profiles about people and sell them to advertisers, spammers, malware distributors, employment agencies, and college admission offices." The researchers explained: "[The] children's merchandise market is in the hundreds of billion dollars in the U.S. alone, it is not surprising that data brokers are already seeking to compile dossiers on children."

We know data brokers compile dossiers on us. But as adults, we often decide which apps to use and how much information to share about *ourselves*. I know that when I agree to the terms on a new app, I rarely think fully about the consequences, and I'm probably one of the more knowledgeable consumers out there. It is scary to think that my actions are giving data brokers information about my *children*.

# Holding Marketers Accountable

As I discussed in chapter one, many countries, including the United States, value parental autonomy. The law rarely steps in to restrict parents from sharing online. Unfortunately, most parents lack the information they need to decide what to share and with whom. Some readers might say that the law *should* step in to protect kids and put the burden on parents not to overshare. But perhaps we can also protect children in a way that doesn't infringe on parental autonomy.

Professors Mariea Hoy and Alexa Fox suggest that websites and corporations should bear some responsibility for PII shared by parents, since they profit most from these disclosures. In their article "Smart Devices, Smart Decisions? Implications of Parents' Sharenting for Children's Online Privacy: An Investigation of Mothers," Hoy and Fox explored how mothers experience a mix of excitement and uncertainty with the birth of a child and how those emotions could lead to oversharing.[48] The researchers noted that following the birth of a child, parents (in this study, mothers) are a particularly vulnerable group of consumers, and as a group, they are often taken advantage of by marketers seeking to obtain their personal information and the personal information of their children.

The mothers Fox and Hoy interviewed had *privacy concerns* when it came to online sharing, but these concerns rarely led to the parents creating *privacy rules*. The researchers found that the mothers were concerned with not posting anything that made them look like bad parents and were also careful to not post anything that could upset or embarrass their children in the future. Of course, these are good first steps, but unfortunately, these concerns do little to protect the child's PII, which could lead to unintended consequences down the road.

The researchers did not place blame on the mothers for over-sharing. Instead, Fox and Hoy suggested that perhaps a better path forward would be to place responsibility on the marketers to either stop encouraging parents to disclose personal information, or if they did ask parents to share, to ensure that parents were first given tools to make informed decisions.[49] These recommendations nicely situate themselves with what my research has also revealed—that most parents have their children's best interests at heart, and society can do a better job at restricting third-party access to personal information. Equally important, parents can be educated and empowered to make wise decisions on behalf of their children.


## Are You Worried?

I asked parents in my online parenting group if they had ever worried about pictures being shared online or being stolen and used by those who might want to harm their kids. I focused on the risk of people stealing for one particular purpose, and I imagine the answers would be much broader had I opened up the question to all of the risks that sharing creates.


Question: Do you worry about pictures you share being stolen and used by pedophiles? If not, has the awful thought that a pedophile could steal your child's image ever crossed your mind? (Sorry for totally freaking you out if you've never considered it!)

- Yes. No pics in bathing suits of my kids allowed.

- Yes, a friend of a friend had it happen so it's always at the forefront of my mind.

- I have not considered it. But YUCK!

- I have thought about this, but I don't worry about it. I keep my privacy settings set to friends only, and they can't share my photos without me getting a notification. This doesn't mean someone couldn't use their account to log in and then do a screenshot, but none of my photos are suggestive or the type I would imagine pedophiles would use, but then again, people are sick and you never know what they could be used for.

- Yes, I've thought of it, and no, I didn't used to worry, but now that she's getting older I do worry.

- Yes, this thought has crossed my mind (unfortunately).

- Yes, I have considered it, which is why I never post on Twitter and only use private accounts, but yeah, I get that that's a possibility...hope that it doesn't happen...like identity theft or credit card fraud. You do the best you can with the tools you have available.

- Unless someone I know personally is a pedophile and I don't know about it, hopefully no pedophile can get his/her hands on a picture of my kiddo because I only accept friends on social media that I know personally.

- I've thought of pedophiles watching or taking video, etc., in public but not much stealing from social media.

- Yes, which is why I am pretty conservative with my posts and who I allow to follow me.

- Yes, that has crossed my mind, all my accounts are private and fairly locked down. I also don't post images of my children without clothes on.

- A horrific thought, but that is responsible for my concern about posting topless photos of little girls. I understand that pedophiles' interests are not that specific, but those type of photos seem the most concerning for me and are easy to control.

- Yes, I've worried about it. I've never posted a naked or partially naked photo of my children. My family has been affected by sexual abuse before my daughters were born so I've been extra careful.

- I don't have my profile public, so I think there's less chance of that happening. I have thought of it before, but I don't worry about it too much.

- Yes. We never post nudity or pictures that could easily be construed as suggestive.

- No. I don't want my photos to be used in that manner, obviously, but I also know that some things are out of my control and it doesn't affect me or my family if some stranger does gross things. Somewhat off topic, but years ago I published a book of knitting patterns for socks. The photos in the book are, of course, all pictures of feet wearing socks. Apparently, there is a thriving online community for foot fetishists. These photos occasionally get passed around in such communities. There was nothing sexual or provocative about the photos (we didn't purposefully pose the feet in sexy ways, whatever that would be). My point is—ANYTHING can be used inappropriately. Any photo that is shared online, but also anytime you go in public some stranger could see you/your kids and either take a photo without you knowing or just take a snapshot in their memory. I don't particularly want to dwell on what some people might be doing with those images, but thankfully I don't have to. There are enough things to worry about that I CAN control, I don't need to spend time worrying about the gross things other people get up to.

- It does and I try to keep my account private and not share "public," also careful about images shared.

- I hadn't thought about it much, and yes, it freaks me out a little, but not near as much as the possibility of someone actually touching my child inappropriately.

- That's pretty much the main reason we don't post pictures of our children. The other reason being that Facebook owns all posted pictures.

- I keep myself up at night thinking about this very thing.

- No, because I don't share any pictures of my children publicly.

- Yes, it has crossed my mind. I don't share bath photos for this reason.

- The awful thought has crossed my mind plenty. We only post pics fully clothed. Otherwise, I can't stress too much about it. My husband and I have privacy settings and are only friends with people we know. A pedophile could take their pictures in public just as easily.

- It's crossed my mind, but again, I try to be very careful about what is available beyond my circle of direct friends.

- Not really, only because I share mostly on Facebook and I have my profile set to private. My Instagram is public though and that thought does totally freak me out (going to switch it to private now!)

I've spent much of the past two years researching how innocent images could be stolen and turned into child pornography. It all started when I was contacted by a reporter from Canada doing a story on how pedophiles were finding innocent images of children online and using them for illicit purposes. I was surprised that the respected reporter called *me* for an interview—surely there were more qualified experts on the subject. But what I learned is that this is an emerging issue for law enforcement personnel around the globe, and unfortunately, policy-makers and scholars have been slow to keep up with the horrific ways criminals are trying to take advantage of children online.

As I delved deeper into the research, I found that there were links between some of the new forms of child pornography and my work in the sharenting realm. Parents posting pictures of their kids were unknowingly creating opportunities for images to be reused and reshared for purposes wholly different than their initial intent. Writing for the *National Post*, one of Canada's leading news publications, Sharon Kirkey discussed this phenomenon: "Pedophiles are re-posting innocuous photos of children lifted from their parents' Facebook accounts, a perverse phenomenon highlighting the darker side of 'sharenting,' those hunting online predators warn."[50] According to the head of Canada's online child pornography hotline, images are often reshared on pedophile websites, where photos of children doing "normal" things are categorized and shared.[51] The issue is affecting children worldwide. The Children's Safety Commissioner of Australia reported that about 50 percent of all images on one pedophile image-sharing site—with at least 45 million images—originated on social media and family blogs.[52]

## Morphed Child Pornography

Not only can images be saved and shared, but they also can be saved and later used to create new obscene images of children. Child welfare experts and law enforcement personnel have traditionally thought child pornography entailed children being sexually abused and recorded at the same time. However, technology now makes it possible for criminals to create a new type of child pornography. Sadly, once images are stolen from a parent's social media feed, they can be obscenely altered using photo editing software. These images, which often combine an innocent image of a child with an image of an individual in a sexualized position, are known as morphed child pornography.[53]

Having images that show real children being sexually abused is a crime under both federal and state law.[54] But what about innocent images of children that get "morphed" to create child pornography? The law is slowly catching up with this dark side of technology.[55, 56] Technology has changed, and child pornography today can look like child pornography of the past, yet not actually be an image of a child being sexually abused.

To protect children from this computer technology and other harms, Congress enacted the Prosecutorial Remedies and Other Tools to End the Exploitation of Children Today Act of 2003 (PROTECT Act).[57] This Act prohibits *all* obscene images that depict children, regardless of whether a child was abused in the image's creation.[58] Federal courts are upholding convictions for possession of these types of images, but some state courts, in states where legislatures have been slow to update their laws, are not.[59]

# A Better Way Forward

While the idea of image theft and morphed child pornography is concerning, the scope of the problem isn't clear. Most published articles mention image theft in passing, and only a handful of cases discuss morphed child pornography, so the evidence of its prevalence is mostly anecdotal. Research shows that there are a few simple steps you can take to protect your children's privacy from the risks discussed in this chapter.

These tips won't fully keep your family safe from predators and data thieves. However, they can give your kids a bit of protection as you continue to stay connected online.

## Takeaways for Staying Safe When Sharing Online

- **Double- (and Triple-) Check Your Privacy Settings.** Social media giants like Facebook have gotten into trouble for sharing our personal information, even after we've taken the time to lock down our settings. For example, in 2018, users were alerted that when the "show as" feature, something designed to help us see what others could see when they visited our timelines, was used, our information became public, causing a major data breach to take place. When we use social media, we need to remember that no matter how careful we are, we can't be sure the website is also taking proper precautions, and therefore our data can get out to a much larger audience than we anticipate.

  That said, there are some steps we can take to give us at least partial protection. I choose to create separate lists on

Facebook—using the "Close Friends" and "Acquaintance" features already built into the platform. When I share pictures of my kids, I usually use the "Close Friends" option, unless it is something that I would be comfortable with even strangers seeing. Even when I do this, I have to keep in mind that I really don't know where the picture could end up. Any image shared online can be stolen and repurposed.

I'm often uncomfortable (and I know that my kids may also be) when I am out in the community and someone comments on or even compliments my kids' achievements, telling me they saw them on Facebook. I know they mean well, but it is a good reminder that people read and remember what I put online. The information is accumulating and giving friends and acquaintances lots of information about our family. If you are anything like me, your Facebook memories go back years and years, and while it is awesome seeing those memories every morning, it is also a reminder of the extent of my children's digital footprints.

I like to go through my pictures every few months, and while I delete some of the pictures, on others I change the privacy setting to "Only Me." This gives me the benefit of having a digital scrapbook and also some peace of mind of having fewer pictures in the semipublic space of my social media feed. It's not perfect, and arguably I should keep all of their pictures offline as some of my more cautious friends do. The "Only Me" setting is only as good as Facebook itself, and I act with the awareness that Facebook's policies can and do change often (and that Facebook is known for data breaches), but it does offer me some semblance of control. I sometimes invite my oldest son to join me when I go back and review old posts, and I've noticed he now does the same on his Instagram feed.

▶ **Don't Share Details.** When it comes to our personal lives, *what* we choose to share is as important than *where* or *how often* we share. We know that data brokers take an interest in learning about our kids. We can make it a bit more challenging for them to do so by not sharing our child's full name or date of birth on a regular basis. Sometimes I do call my children by their first names on social media, but I try to call them by a nickname or an initial when I can. I like to post happy birthday messages (not only to share with friends, but so that I can see them when I look back in future years), but I recognize that by doing so, I'm sharing a bit more than I'm regularly comfortable with, so sometimes I do it a day before or a day after the actual birthday. And I rarely include their names in the birthday post.

▶ **Don't Post Naked Pictures.** It's amazing how often I come across naked toddler bath pictures online. Sure, when it's your own kiddo, it is super cute. Often, the picture is posed in such a way that no privates are shown, and then it's even super cute when I don't know the kid. But these pictures are prime targets for pedophiles.

▶ **Tell Friends, Family, School, and Community Organizations about Your Sharing Preferences.** As a children's privacy researcher, I always ask my friends before posting a picture of their child online. I'm often shocked to hear the friend thank me for asking—it turns out, it's not something all people do before sharing pictures of other people's kids online. But it should be commonplace. People should *always* ask before sharing a picture of another person—especially before sharing a picture of another person's child. Some of us have strong preferences, while others have safety concerns. Their safety concerns are valid, and we should respect them even if we still choose to share about our kids.

At the same time, it is up to each of us to express our preferences to those who interact with our kids. Tell your child's school if you are OK with the administration or teachers posting pictures of your child. Ask if they have a policy regarding parent volunteers sharing when they volunteer in the classroom or on a field trip. Talk to your child's coach or religious organization to avoid conflicts before they arise. Being proactive about sharing is much more efficient than having an uncomfortable conversation afterward.

———

It's tempting to just delete our Facebook accounts and vow to only share pictures of our kids with significant others and grandparents, or to start sharing the old-fashioned way, through mail or email or text. But that could make it much more difficult for many who rely on social media to stay connected with family and friends. We have lots of questions, and a long way to go to fully protect our children's privacy online. These tips can serve as a starting point.

## CHAPTER FIVE

# Our Sharenting Mindset— and Theirs

My friends Adam and Michelle have an adorable six-year-old, Jon. Last year, Adam woke up to find Jon working hard on an art project at the kitchen table. As he got closer, his eyes widened. His lips pursed, the corners of his mouth fighting a smile. With each shake of his head, his ability to fight his smile got weaker.

Jon was making flyers. Not just any flyers. Flyers that said, "We will not use curse words in this house." Flyers with words with big red x's in front of them. Words I can't write in this book. Jon had awoken early that morning and found the blank paper and markers. He had gotten in trouble earlier in the week for using curse words, and Jon decided to try to write out the lessons his parents had been reinforcing at home.

And even though I wasn't there, I know all about them. Not because we laughed about it over dinner that night, not because of a great phone call I had that day with Michelle, but because I, along with Adam and Michelle's combined one thousand friends, saw the pictures on their Facebook newsfeed. The post was well received online, garnering likes, comments, and even a few shares from close family.

Jon loved his flyers. He was super proud of them, and he was happy his dad shared them with his online social network.

He certainly would not understand the complexity that surrounded his dad's decision to share. He wouldn't understand that his dad shared it out of pride for his son's creativity, that it filled him with love to see him taking a lesson and making concrete ways for the family to practice it. Jon's a showman at heart, and he loved his dad's reaction and the attention that followed his dad's decision to share. But of course, it won't be until he gets older that he really understands what happened that day in the vast space between the kitchen table and his dad's Facebook newsfeed.

As Jon gets older, he will likely come face-to-face with his dad's online disclosures. Whether he gets a Facebook account of his own or whether he simply scrolls back into his parents' newsfeed, one day he will see the pictures they've shared, the stories they've told. And Adam and Michelle hope he will appreciate this online journal of sorts that they've created.

## Public Attention

I first logged on to Facebook in 2008, and like many of the kids growing up in the decade that followed, my son is part of a cohort of kids that professors Emma Nottingham, Helen James, and Marion Oswald call "Generation Tagged."[60] The professors, by researching kids who appeared on the British television show *The Secret Life of 4, 5 and 6 Year Olds*, explored how early fame affects kids who grow up in the public eye. Their article "The Not-So-Secret Life of Five-Year-Olds: Legal and Ethical Issues Relating to Disclosure of Information and the Depiction of Children on Broadcast and Social Media," focuses on a documentary where children are recorded interacting in a made-for-TV school setting.

While parents had given consent for their children to participate in the documentary, the researchers were concerned that this public exposure could still violate the children's right to privacy. The researchers highlight the need for more oversight to protect children in public spaces. They conclude the article with a message applicable to many of us, whether we share publicly or on private newsfeeds. "As we are beginning to understand the long-term implications of Internet publication, now is the time for us all to step back to consider whether we want private childhood moments to become eternal public entertainment and the subject of social media public comment."

Nottingham is now conducting a study to explore how early childhood fame impacts children as they grow older. As this first generation to grow up shared comes of age, it will be interesting to see how they view the public personas created for them, often without their consent, and possibly with little consideration for their best interests.

Social media adds a unique dimension to what once was simply a rite of passage—a part of growing up under the watchful eyes of parents and grandparents. Today, children grow up before a larger audience, coming of age under the watchful eyes of a parent's newsfeed. We know that children aren't always OK with this. Many children wish their parents would think twice before sharing their private moments on social media.

## How Kids View Online Sharing

Before the age of seven, kids have a hard time differentiating scenarios on television or video from what occurs in real life. By the time kids reach eight or nine, the ability to differentiate reality from simulations becomes more concrete. This is a time when kids might approach social media with skepticism. Sonia Livingstone, one researcher I referenced in chapter two, found that many in this age group were concerned about strangers on social media, and as she reported, "much of their talk reflects what others had told them, often in warning."

As kids approach adolescence, it gets harder to avoid social media. They generate their own experiences online, and while their wariness often grows, so does their desire for independence. This independence, combined with parents continuing to share, can be a recipe for anxiety and embarrassment if we don't keep talking *to* them instead of *at* them. Leading parenting expert Devorah Heitner, PhD, identifies these kids as "digital natives," and as she explains in her book *Screenwise*, these kids want parents to have rules governing the use of technology.[61]

———

ComRes, working in partnership with the BBC, conducted a survey to better understand how families share online.[62] The survey asked children the following questions (and a few others) about their social media use, and the answers were enlightening. The kids surveyed were ages ten through twelve, about half boys and half girls.

▸    **"Which of these words best describe how you feel when** you use social media?" There were 57 percent of the eleven-year-olds who answered "happy."

▶ **"If you didn't have social media, how would you feel?"** There were 28 percent of the twelve-year-olds who answered that they would feel "excluded."

▶ **"When you look at the social media pages of your friends, how do you feel?"** Approximately 10 percent of kids answered "competitive." Almost 10 percent of all eleven-year-olds surveyed answered "jealous."

▶ **"Generally, how important or otherwise is it to look good in selfies that you take?"** The kids were asked about their own social media use, and more than 75 percent of those surveyed (equal amounts of boys and girls) answered that it is either "very important" or "quite important" to look good in the pictures.

▶ **"Do your parents ever post photos of you on their social media?"** Of course, this is where the answers got especially interesting to me, as they really start to focus on what I study. Over 60 percent of the kids surveyed said yes, their parents do post pictures of them on social media.

▶ **"How do you feel about your parents posting photos of you on their social media?"** The researchers asked the kids who answered yes to the last question how they felt about their parents posting, and 31 percent of twelve-year-olds said that it didn't affect them, but 30 percent of the eleven-year-olds said that it made them feel embarrassed. Many of the kids surveyed told the researchers that by sharenting, their parents made them feel either embarrassed, anxious, worried, or sad.

▶ **"Have you ever been unhappy with a photo someone else has posted of you on social media?"** Approximately 25 percent of the kids answered yes. The study went even further. These kids were asked why they felt unhappy, and the most common responses indicated that kids weren't happy with their appearance in the pictures and that the parents "did not ask me before uploading it."

The study found that by age ten, kids had strong reactions to sharenting. Their reactions grew even stronger by age twelve. Children want parents to ask permission before sharing their stories and pictures online.

———

In their article "Not at the Dinner Table: Parents' and Children's Perspectives on Family Technology Rules," Alexis Hiniker and Julie Kientz of the University of Washington and Sarita Schoenebeck of the University of Michigan spoke to 249 parent-child pairs about how they use and monitor social media in their homes.[63] The study reported that "children were twice as likely to report that adults should not 'overshare' by posting information about children online without permission. Children were also significantly more likely to report that adults should be held to the same rules as children and that adults should respect children's autonomy with technology."

Schoenebeck, a leader in the sharenting field, also paired up with Carol Moser and Tianying Chen to write "Parents' and Children's Preferences about Parents Sharing about Children on Social Media."[64] Together, the researchers surveyed over three hundred parent-child pairs to better understand how the families share on social media.

Overall, the team noted that children are generally supportive of their parents posting positive things about them on social media, but they voiced apprehension about parents sharing things that could be viewed as embarrassing or unflattering. The authors recommended that parents involve children in their decision-making process.

———

In my household, terms like flattering/unflattering or cute/ugly are subjective—my thirteen-year-old, for example, loves to wear his curly hair as big and full as possible, whereas I prefer it with a little more control. What I view as handsome, he sees as awful. But when I think back to my own childhood, I still remember clothes shopping with my mom and the two of us having polarized fashion viewpoints. Like I had, he is developing his own sense of self and appreciation for his own image. Most parents I've spoken to would advise, offline at least, for other parents to pick their battles, and in all things style, simply get out of their child's way. As I read the study, it seems that the researchers suggest our social media image is no different—we would be best to allow our children to judge for themselves how a certain image makes them look, because it is likely how they truly feel. This could allow parents to share about their kids in a way that fosters, not inhibits, their relationship.

Schoenebeck, Moser, and Chen found that for the most part, the children surveyed felt that their parents were listening to their preferences and were generally OK with how their parents were sharing. This is reassuring. The authors explained that the children "agree with their parents that parents' frequency of sharing is about right. This suggests that at least some concerns about parent sharing from the perspective of the child may be unwarranted. Furthermore, these results introduce possible benefits of parental sharing, such as building trust between parents and children when preferences are known and increasing self-esteem of the child when parents share positive posts."

—

My friend Jennifer (who is a psychologist) has mastered the art of sharing about parenting while valuing a child's right to privacy. Her oldest daughter, Dawn, is thirteen and has had a boyfriend for about eight months. The pair has made a few appearances on Jennifer's social media newsfeed (with the kids' permission), but Jennifer doesn't use the boyfriend's name or say the two are dating because Dawn has made it clear that she doesn't want extended family to know they are in a relationship. This doesn't just make for a more harmonious mother-daughter relationship, but it's also a lesson in consent.

With both of her children, Jennifer is careful about not posting any group shots of other people's children unless she knows them well and has already gotten their permission. Instead, Jennifer sends the pictures directly to the parents of the other children and lets them know she is OK with them sharing online and tagging her family. By doing so, she hopes that she is setting a standard that will guide other parents when they share her family's pictures online.

———

Schoenebeck, Moser, and Chen's study[65] concluded with recommendations on how social media sites could use technology to better embrace their findings. For example, the authors suggested design options such as an "Okay to Post" feature, encouraging parents to tag their children to "approve or disapprove a post and select a dropdown reason why. The parent would learn the child's preferences in a supportive and non-confrontational manner."

Moser, Chen, and Schoenebeck further suggest that social media sharing sites could use technology to better understand what kids generally prefer parents not share. This could "capture the pulse of children's evolving preferences." Lastly, the researchers suggest that social media sites could use technology to identify the tone of a parent's post. "Posts could be scanned for positive or negative text/expressions," the authors explain, "and when negative, the user could be given a prompt asking if they really want to share this."

## Ages and Stages

I asked my parenting group if they ask their children before posting about them online. I also asked if there is an age at which parents should start asking their kids before posting about them online. There didn't seem to be much of a consensus, but a clear pattern emerged. Parents understand that it is important to ask older kids before sharing about them online; however, they struggled to define the appropriate age at which they should begin posing the question.

**Question: Do you ask your children before posting about them online? Is there an age where you think parents should start asking children before posting about them online?**

- I do not post him online, because at three, he is too young to provide his consent.

- I think twelve is the appropriate age to start asking them.

- Yes, I ask. Mostly my twelve-year-old. The eight-year-old I don't worry about as much.

- Mine is too young, but I think start asking when they can answer questions and keep asking as they grow and start to learn more complexity.

- I've started to ask my daughters more often (age eight and twelve).

- No, I don't ask. But with that said, my seven-year-old is starting to be more "in the know" about social media, so I think when they are old enough to be aware, we should ask.

- My kids are too young to ask but I don't post much.

- It depends on the child. I don't ask my under-five kids.

- No. I think I will ask my son soon (he is almost six).

- I don't ask at this point, kids aged three and a half and one. If they start asking what I am doing and seem bothered by it, I will start to consider their feelings and ask what they would prefer.

- I do not currently, but with my oldest turning five tomorrow, I will probably do so shortly.

- My kids are too young, but I think when they turn six or seven and understand social media, I'll start asking for their permission.

- I don't yet. My children are four and two. Maybe when she has a better understanding of what "online" means.

- Yes! Consent should just be a standard part of life!

- No, because my oldest is only three. He is already aware that we share photos and videos with family members online though and will ask me to take a picture of him doing something (or a new toy) to send to Grandma.

- No. He's not old enough to talk yet. Probably should start asking when they start school.

- I do not as my children are very young, but I would respect their privacy as they got older and requested I not share photos or details of their lives.

- I don't. I rarely post anything. And only people they know see the posts and I never use their names. I also remove information from the photos I post and I never turn on location on my phone if I use photos from a phone.

- Yes. I believe I started to ask their opinion around fifth grade. My daughters don't have Facebook but scroll my newsfeed. We began discussing why people post. My oldest, now fourteen, asked probably three years ago—why do we need to know about every softball hit a friend made? We laughed but it led to many family discussions about matters like this.

- Not yet. But I'm careful not to post anything that would be upsetting or embarrassing to them later. We always ask my nine-year-old nephew if it's OK because he wants to approve pics—so probably around then?

- No, I don't ask, but I also don't post material that would embarrass them in any way or that is derogatory.

- Sometimes for my nine-year-old, but more often, he tells me to "post that on Facebook" even when I don't think it's appropriate. For the five-year-old, I don't ask but will likely do so once he is a bit older and understands time/permanency better.

As a group, the parents I questioned agreed that at a certain point, kids should have veto power over their parents' online disclosures. But when the time comes and kids do start to assert their independence, it can be difficult to always honor their requests.

## Kids Want Control

We are seeing this conflict play out when we see the children of celebrities in the news get upset about what their parents post online. While watching their family drama might be funny, I can't help but wonder how many other teens who don't have a similar platform wish they'd had a voice in what and how their parents share. When Gwyneth Paltrow shared a picture of herself and her daughter, Apple, skiing in early 2019, Apple responded, "Mom, we have discussed this. You may not post anything without my consent."[66] Gwyneth seemed to take it in stride, and it's hard to tell if Apple really was disturbed, but the story was enough to capture a lot of attention, with plenty of commentators weighing in during the post's aftermath.

In an article discussing the growing resentment of teenagers whose entire lives have been showcased on social media, Joanne Orlando, a professor at Western Sydney University, told the *Guardian*, "They don't have any control over what their parents are putting up, or what comments their parents are adding to photos or videos, but we all know our digital lives are increasingly important. So they want to gain control over it when they're able to."[67] She explained that while in the United Kingdom there haven't been cases where children have sued their parents for oversharing, the growing discomfort could cause more of a backlash within families and within the law. Orlando highlighted that in France, parents can face fines and even jail time for oversharing about their children online. All over the world, parents and policy-makers are struggling to find a balance between a parent's right to share and a child's right to privacy.

## Vulnerable Children

Writer Phoebe Maltz Bovy has voiced concern that parents are potentially exploiting their children through the public disclosure of personal information in online forums.[68] She has attempted to define the concept of *oversharing* to criticize parents' use of social media that goes beyond sharing to exploitation of their own children.[69] In her article "The Ethical Implications of Parents Writing about Their Kids," Bovy explores whether children can *ever* give consent for online disclosure of personal, potentially harmful, and embarrassing information. She states, "The reader assumes that the parent will do what's best for her child. While the parent may set out to do this, using their own children in the service of a larger argument clouds their ability to self-censor. And with confession can come vanity."

The power of a mother's voice is incredible—but it can also be damaging. Like with so many decisions we make as parents, there isn't a one-size-fits-all balance. Consider one mother's essay, "I Am Adam Lanza's Mother."[70] After twenty-year-old Adam Lanza killed twenty children and six faculty members at Sandy Hook Elementary School in 2012, this woman (who is not Adam Lanza's mother) wrote an impassioned essay expressing her struggle raising a mentally ill son. In the article, she pleaded for mental health reform, stating, "I am sharing this story because I am Adam Lanza's mother. I am Dylan Klebold's and Eric Harris's mother. I am James Holmes's mother. I am Jared Loughner's mother. I am Seung-Hui Cho's mother. And these boys—and their mothers—need help. In the wake of another horrific national tragedy, it's easy to talk about guns. But it's time to talk about mental illness."

By sharing her own story, and the story of her thirteen-year-old son, this mother graphically and bravely expressed the catastrophic challenges of raising a mentally ill and violent child. She included her own name and a picture of her son, and she described her daily parenting struggles. By expressing herself, perhaps this mother offered a much-needed reality check to politicians and others at the forefront of public discourse on childhood mental health. Yet at the same time, she disclosed very personal, private information about her child to the world. Thus, it can be very difficult to differentiate advocacy from oversharing.

———

What can we glean from the research, and how can we use it to make better online sharing decisions in the future?

First, parental autonomy is a fundamental principle of our society. In most circumstances, parents are best able to make decisions for their own families, and while the law could regulate sharenting in extreme cases, in the normal course, few would suggest that parents not be permitted to share about their children online. However, there are those who disagree. Some countries have passed laws limiting what information parents can share online about their children. Like I mentioned in the last section,

France has privacy laws that would in essence prohibit parents from over-sharenting.[71] While I've been unable to locate a specific law that explicitly covers interfamilial privacy, France's strict privacy laws would apparently apply if parents share personal information about their kids. "[French authorities] have warned parents in France they could face fines...and a year in prison for publishing intimate photos of their children on social media without permission, as part of the country's strict privacy laws," writes Nicole Kobie in the *Guardian*.[72]

Kids have always been embarrassed by what their parents share with family and friends, but by sharing on social media, the information will remain long after the initial disclosure is made. Online revelations can exist for years into the future and could show themselves in a variety of ways over the course of a child's life.

———

Parents must concern themselves not only with how a parenting story might affect a child's well-being today but also how such a disclosure could affect a child years into the future. This is challenging to reconcile with the great support network social media also offers. I, along with many other parents, benefit by sharing our stories online. We've created new communities, connected with faraway family members and friends, and advocated for far-reaching and critical support that benefits families, children, and communities alike. We find help on social media when our children are struggling, and we offer advice when our friends are in need. Parents who have shared online have offered me support and encouragement and have made me feel less isolated when I've faced my own struggles. I've felt more confident and supported when I've shared online about my kids.

## Balancing Interests

I am a clinical law professor, and through my teaching, I represent abused and neglected children in court proceedings. I stand before the court as the child's attorney. On any given day, to my left stands the attorney for the Department of Children and Families ("the state"), to my immediate right usually stands attorneys for the parents, and on the far side of the courtroom is the child's guardian *ad litem* attorney. We all stand before the court with different interests, but likely all stand there representing our client's view of what is best for them. The state made the decision to remove the child from the home; the parent, in most cases, believes he or she is able to meet the child's needs and that the child should come home; the guardian *ad litem* advocates for what he or she believes is best for the child; and I argue for what the child actually wants.

As you can imagine, the judge usually gives a lot of weight to what the state says and strongly considers the guardian *ad litem*'s position. But she also strongly considers the position of the parents, and she always wants to hear from me, voicing the expressed wishes of the child. She sifts through this information and ultimately decides what is best for the child in each decision she makes. There is a reason *she* makes the decision, not the guardian *ad litem*, and not the state. Because while they are tasked with acting in the child's best interest, our laws make it clear that in order to really determine what is best, we need to listen to *everyone's* perspective, even if the perspective isn't a popular one. Even if the perspective is an immature one. Even if the perspective is a quiet one that isn't used to being heard. Only then can the court make a truly informed decision.[73]

When we share about our kids, we are acting like the judge. Most of the time, this is the same position as the guardian *ad litem*. We are often acting in what we think is in our child's best interest. But in the uniquely original situation—where we both benefit from sharing our child's stories and are the ones tasked with protecting their interest—there can often lie a conflict of interest. There is no judge or jury to tell us what to share. It's up to us to play devil's advocate. It's up to us to listen to our children's voices, even if we must help them find their words.

## The Conversation

Talking to kids about how we share isn't rocket science, but it can be challenging to find the words when we are trying to explain social media to young kids. I've decided to ask my kids if they are OK with me sharing their picture. I've gotten better at this over the past few years. If I have their buy-in before the camera comes out, they are relaxed and happier. Sometimes, when I put them in control, they will even ask me to take certain pictures, and what could have been a painful exchange becomes much more fun.

We know that when we take a picture, it will likely be viewed again (by us and likely others), but kids don't necessarily understand why we are pointing our phones in their faces when they are totally immersed in an activity. Taking a moment to ask first often makes me think a bit deeper about my own motivations to whip out the camera. I know that by asking (and taking the picture),

I will be forcing my child to step away mentally from whatever activity she is fully present in. Do I really want to take her out of the moment? Do I really want to take myself out of it?

Often, the answer is no, and the camera ends up staying tucked away into my bag. Instead, I make a mental note of the magical moment I was about to record, reminding myself that it's the feeling of the moment, not the image capturing the moment, I so desperately want to hold on to.

## Takeaways for Inviting Kids into the Sharing Conversation

▶ **Ask them first.** Devorah Heitner, PhD, explains in her book *Screenwise* that by asking your kids for permission before posting about them, you are teaching them valuable lessons, like self-control, respect, and empowerment.[74] Heitner also explains that by asking first, we are helping to create a respectful relationship with our kids. "Your child will have a better understanding of this complex social media exchange... because you've modeled it," she writes. She highlights that this will help kids make better decisions on their own when navigating social media's tough terrain. "Talk to your child about how your respect for her makes her feel and urge her to think about how others feel when she's the one taking pictures of her friends," Heitner writes.

▶ **Start young.** It's easy to write off the opinions of little kids when sharing online. After all, chances are your three-year-old has no clue what Facebook is. My own six-year-old adorably calls it "the Facebook," and sometimes when she catches me scrolling, she wants to sit and scroll with me. "Who's that?" she asked as I clicked on a photo this past weekend. It happened to be her cousin. My scrolling turned into a family tree lesson, and by the time we finished talking, my iPhone had gone dim.

▶ **Keep your opinions to yourself.** Usually by the time I'm asking my kids if they are OK with my sharing of their photo, I've already made up my mind that I *really* want to share it. After all, I'm the sharenting researcher, and I overthink *everything.* By the time I'm asking, my heart is already set.

Despite the wishes of my heart, I know I need to put on my poker face when asking them how they feel about me sharing the picture. If I want to really tap into their anxiety, embarrassment, or uncertainty, it's critical that I not allow their emotions to be hampered by my own excitement. I need to own my role in influencing their decisions and offer my opinions sparingly when gauging their comfort with me sharing their stories. There will be times I disagree with their preferences, but I want them to have a general sense that I value their autonomy and I value their feelings with respect to privacy.

▶ **Share feedback with your kids but limit its scope.** The conversation shouldn't end the moment a picture enters your newsfeed. As your phone pushes notifications of comments, likes, and loves, share these responses with your children *within reason.* It is helpful for kids to understand what happens after a photo is shared. At the same time, kids can quickly develop a warped sense of self if they become reliant on social media feedback.[75] We see this with our tweens and teens, but by allowing younger kids to engage online through our newsfeeds, we may be setting them up early for the same issues. Hopefully, we can curtail this by turning off the push notifications and instead waiting a few hours to review the feedback all at once, in one sitting. This could put it into perspective and allow our younger children to better appreciate the limited role social media should play in our everyday experiences.

▶ **Review old posts at least once a year.** Some social media sites make it difficult to change your privacy settings in bulk, and therefore changing the audience for individual photos on your newsfeed can be burdensome and time-consuming. However, a digital footprint can grow quickly, and I find it is helpful to review old posts at least once a year to avoid the task becoming insurmountable. While little kids probably have no interest in sitting through the mind-numbing process of cleaning up a newsfeed, older kids might appreciate the chance to review old disclosures and may feel empowered to call the shots when it comes to their deletion.

While social media isn't the best way to create a personal timeline, many parents relish the memory feature it offers. Some parents I spoke with pull from their social media feed when making photo albums and gifts each year. Privacy risks certainly remain when we share photos on Facebook, even if the audience is public or set to "Only Me." But the "Only Me" and "Close Friends" settings allow parents to feel slightly more in control of their family's growing footprint. When kids ask for deletion, most parents talk to their kids about their preferences, and hopefully they honor their requests. While our kids may not fully comprehend social media's implications, as they get older, our efforts can help them understand the nuances and complexities presented by our online social networks.

CHAPTER SIX:

# Altering the Lens of Our Experiences

Writing for the New York Times, Julia Cho explored whether our constant recording (and more importantly, our constant sharing) of our children's everyday accomplishments may be affecting how they recall and reflect on their experiences.[76] Cho's mother had recorded her granddaughter's part in the school talent show, and after the event was over, offered to play it back for the child. Cho, sensing that perhaps it was best not to replay the video so close in time to the event, asked her mother not to show the child the video just yet. Her hesitancy, Cho later learned, had some scientific basis. When we create memories, they are based on our own experiences. Watching a video too soon after an experience can fundamentally change the experience for us.

Nadine Davidson-Wall highlighted this concern in her paper "'Mum, Seriously!': Sharenting the New Social Trend with No Opt-out."[77] As we create curated versions of childhood, we risk altering our own memories, and likely the memories of our children. Davidson-Wall explains, "The public presentation of selective and edited photos of children, controlled by parents, shapes the memory of these children, influencing self-definition." When we are constantly documenting childhood, we are, in some ways, rewriting childhood. Childhood memories *should* be based on our perceptions as minors, right? I want my five-year-old to remember the first time she went to Disney World on *her own* terms. I don't want her to grow up having it defined by the curated view I chose to put in my newsfeed.

———

Earlier this month, I took a picture of a friend's daughter receiving an award. After the main event but while the families were still socializing, I went up to the friend, turned on my camera, and tried to show the little girl the photograph. "It's OK," my friend said. "She can see it later."

I get so excited by my camera, by the images I capture, that sometimes I all too quickly escape the moment and think about the image I want to edit in Lightroom, when I get home. My friend's comment was an excellent reminder to just put it away. To be excited for the moment, not for the memory. To not damage our children's view of this moment with the image as captured by my camera's lens.

## Stay in the Moment, Not in the Newsfeed

KJ Dell'Antonia, author of *How to Be a Happier Parent,* wrote an eye-opening essay for the *New York Times* titled "Facebook Is Stealing Your Family's Joy."[78] In the article, Dell'Antonia suggests that as we've become more aware of the drawbacks of sharing our lives on social media, we've become more cautious about posting our day-to-day moments online. Quoting professor Julianna Miner, Dell'Antonia writes, "'It takes something like six virtual hugs to equal one real hug.' Time spent seeking those virtual hugs can take us outside the world we're living in, and draw us back to our phones (which, of course, is the reason many networks offer those bursts of feedback in the first place)." Dell'Antonia reached out to me for a quote as she wrote this article, but it was I who benefited from the conversation. Dell'Antonia shifted my thinking, altering the lens through which I view my own work as a scholar, and my most important work as a mom.

———

Social media takes us away from interactions with the people right in front of us. When we choose to share an accomplishment online, we've lost the chance to share it in person with the people we care most about. And when we go back to our post to see who has liked or commented, we are momentarily escaping from the real world. To our kids, these momentary escapes amount to multitudes of moments where we are not fully present, moments where we've traded in our actual world to exist in a virtual one.

And I'd venture to guess that in those moments, we aren't only missing things, but the people we care most about are missing us.

———

It's hard for today's young parents to imagine a time before families were connected online. Whether through an email or a via a status update, we now know more information about more people in our offline networks than ever before. An old-fashioned game of "telephone tag" might have shared birth news faster than relying only on snail-mail birth announcements, but even *that* naturally limited the spread of information. Today we are inundated with information that, over the long term, may be far more information than our minds can make sense of. Our innate desire to create meaningful connections can quickly become overwhelmed by the connectivity at our fingertips, and our ability to separate the meaning-*ful* from the meaning-*less* is getting hampered. This isn't because we have meaningless information on our newsfeed. We just have *so much* information at our fingertips that it's hard to keep up with all our "friends." Is the quality of our relationships suffering due to the quantity of relationships our social media networks encourage us to have?

For those of us who thrive on connectedness, social media is often exhausting. My friend Sara struggles with this exhaustion, especially when multiple people in her newsfeed seem to need attention all at once. When Sara hears of someone in need, she not only opens her wallet but also actively helps friends problem solve. Sara is the kind of confidant we all want to have—and thanks to social media, over one thousand friends get to claim her as one of their own. "I love knowing my network is vast," Sara told me. "But with this connectivity comes a sense of obligation. When a distant friend posts an update saying her family needs help, I feel a moral obligation to step in. It's overwhelming, and my online interactions feel more like obligations to help than opportunities to connect," she told me.

## How Will This Information Affect Our Children Today?

Consider how your child will feel when they walk into school, church, or other activities in the days after you share something personal. After the rioting and deadly attack at a white supremacist rally in Charlottesville, Virginia, in 2017, I chose to share my family's story of surviving the Holocaust during an interview with Allison Slater Tate, a writer for *Today* Parents.[79] The story ran alongside pictures of my children and grandparents. My kids loved the feature, but I think my oldest child was a bit surprised by the publicity. He was still processing what happened, and since the article was shared widely, he was often asked about it. Our son's math teacher shared the article with the class, using it as a springboard for their classroom discussion. His soccer coach commented about how brave his great-grandparents were. The younger two kids each wanted to print out a copy of the article and bring it to their classes. It was an empowering experience but also an overwhelming one. For some kids, it also could have caused a lot of anxiety. Did I make the right decision in allowing our family to be featured? I think so, but I can see why some would disagree with me.

———

Joy, a family-focused sharer I mentioned in chapter two, has to worry that if she shares too much, her kids could be harmed, something that briefly crossed my mind when I allowed our story to be featured in front of such a potentially large audience. "Because of the lines of work my husband and I do, I tend to be cautious of potential predators online and also the ability to track down my family through things I post," Joy explained when

I asked her why she tended to hesitate. She is a prosecutor, and her husband works in the medical field. "While people know my address, I don't advertise it on my feed. I do sometimes reference the kids' schools. I don't use their teachers' names or anything else that could be used by someone to 'prove' to the kids that they are a friend. The kids know not to go with anyone and not to give any personal info to strangers."

Along with having concerns about safety, Joy also avoids sharing anything negative on social media. "I try to post accomplishments and funny things but nothing about them getting in trouble or anything that could be construed as a poor reflection on them." Joy is a personal friend of mine, and she told me that a lot of the reasoning behind her actions "is actually because of the conversations you and I have had," she told me (causing me to blush), "and the subsequent reading I've done."

## How Will This Information Affect Our Children When They Get Older?

Sometimes we share with the confidence that our child will never see our disclosure. Sure, that might be the case, but unfortunately, we never really know what happens with our information once we put it on social media. Our kids might access it or hear about it, and it's important that we think through how that could affect them. We all have some values that we feel strongly enough about to scream from the rooftops. Many of us hold certain foundational ideals about religion or morality that we are confident putting our children's names behind, even if they do not hold those values themselves. In those cases, a parent might choose to take a family

stand online without talking to their kids, or perhaps even disre-
garding their wishes. But as Jeffrey Shulman states, "The expres
sive liberty of parents becomes despotic when the child is given
no real opportunity to embrace other values and to believe other
beliefs."[80] The information we share online, no matter how altruis-
tically, about our children or about our family's experiences could
quickly become the online identity of the child years into the future.

———

Berman and Albright, two researchers I mentioned in chapter four,
set off to answer this question. They write, "In an era of increasing
dependence on data science and big data, the voices of one set of
major stakeholders—the world's children and those who advocate on their behalf—have been largely absent." Yet despite their
absence, children are significantly impacted by the collection of
their data.

Berman and Albright highlight prior research suggesting that
the biggest impact of data sharing regarding children is not just
the dissemination of that data in the moments it is shared, but also
its accumulation over a child's life.[81] It's possible, the researchers
explain, that information shared by others during a child's young
life could be greater than information the child would ever share.
This means that who our children become "online" as young adults
is more of a reflection of our impressions of them rather than their
impressions of themselves. We want our children to self-actualize
and become independent. While we may want them to share our
values and maybe follow in some of our footsteps, ultimately, we
want them to make these decisions on their own. In short, we want
them to be themselves, not miniature versions of us.

## Takeaways for Staying Connected Offline When Sharing Online

▶ **Wait to share.** Don't share while the moment is still happening. Don't even think about sharing until the moment has passed and you've shifted gears entirely. By allowing the experience to stay authentic and in the offline world, you can give yourself time to process it without interpretation or commentary by your newsfeed friends.

▶ **Step away from the feedback loop.** Sometimes, it is helpful to consider your motivations for sharing. Is it because you want feedback or is it so that you'll have the memory pop up this time next year? If it's the latter, consider downloading an app like 1 Second Everyday that collects memories and creates a personal picture/video diary of your week, month, or year.[82] You could also do what one good friend of mine does and always post using the "Only Me" setting on Facebook. This will allow you to see your pictures in your memories, ideally without showing them on your newsfeed. I say *ideally* because social networking sites like Facebook are notorious for data breaches. It's possible when that happens, anything you shared in the past with a smaller audience could end up shared publicly without your consent.[83]

▶ **Talk to your family and friends who choose not to share at all.** Remember the oppositional social media users and non-users mentioned in chapter two? You surely have some of these people in your life. Take a moment to walk in their shoes and ask them why they've chosen to restrict sharing. They might offer you new ideas for how to best cross the intersection of sharing online and keeping a clear perspective of the view ahead.

———

We've come a long way since our first social media disclosures a little over a decade ago. We know what we've lost by oversharing—closeness, privacy, and maybe even joy. I think we are at a crossroads. We know what this social media revolution has taken away from our lives, but many of us are still drawn to its shine. We still love the drug-like rush we get after posting a picture and awaiting feedback, but we are now aware that by oversharing, we run the risk of altering the lens through which we see the world.

## CHAPTER SEVEN

# Helping Ourselves and Our Kids Share Better

Like most parents of young kids, I get some great gifts designed by tiny hands at school. Last year, for Mother's Day, there were drawings, poems, handprints, and sculptures. There were "I love you" messages and "You make me happy when we read together" love notes. My eight-year-old made a lovely book for me. There must have been twenty messages that made me melt. But there was one that made me cringe.

The teacher's writing prompt said: *Mommy always has...*

My eight-year old's answer was: *her phone.*

In that moment I wanted to throw the phone across the room and cry. All the loving notes, all the pictures and messages about how much he liked reading with me, how much he thought I liked playing basketball with him, how much he loved my big soft arms hugging him before bedtime.

I felt like a complete and utter failure. In my child's eyes, I always had my phone with me.

You might be shaking your head at me, silently judging, but I know I'm not alone. Other parents also have trouble putting the phone away. Here are some of the answers I received from my Facebook group.

**Question: How do you try to model appropriate smartphone and social media use for your children?**

- Unfortunately, this is an area I need to improve vastly on as I'm guilty of being on it far too much.

- I do a bad job at that.

- I think we are all on our phones too much!

- I need to work on this. We do put phones away for one-on-one time, meals, etc.

- I have not thought about this but will now.

- Working on being present and not on my phone while playing with them. It's a work in progress!

- It's hard some days, but I try to stay off my phone once I am home with the kids in the afternoon.

- When I'm around my kids, I try to stay off my phone as much as possible but I'm a work in progress. It's addictive. I'll check

my work email or answer a text, but I try to be present in the
moment when I'm at home with my girls.

- I don't think I model social media use for them yet because they
  are so young.

- [I ask] permission before I post images or stories. Not just asking
  my children, also asking my friends and family.

- Like most parents I try not to overuse screens, but I do an awful
  job at it.

- I try to not be interacting with the phone when I am interacting
  with them.

- Try to put it away when they're talking to me.

- Lots of eye contact and I set my phone to turn off after I've been
  online for an hour in case I forget.

## Digital Citizenship

In their article "Digital Citizenship: Addressing Appropriate
Technology Behavior," Mike Ribble, Gerald Bailey, and Tweed
Ross explain that digital citizenship "can be defined as the
norms of behavior with regard to technology use."[84] Their article was published in conjunction with the International Society
for Technology in Education (ISTE) and sets forth standards for

teaching kids ages five through eighteen about technology. While the report is designed to show how technology can be modeled and taught in the classroom, it is also an excellent framework for parents to consider when covering digital citizenship with their own children.

## Using Our Phones at Appropriate Times

While I am pretty good about putting my phone away when I go out to lunch with friends, I struggle to model good technology etiquette at home. The people who need me to be a strong role model often see me at my worst. Since beginning to write this book, I have been trying to do better. Ribble and his colleagues suggest that the best way to teach etiquette is to model it at home. Not using our phones when we are interacting is a good place to start. Being polite in our texts is another. When parenting younger kids, it's the presence of the phone, not the substance of what we are doing with it, that is the root problem. Young kids don't understand the difference between checking our phone because we are "on call" for work or checking it for social media status updates. I waste way too much time trying to explain to my youngest child *why* I'm on my phone, as if providing her with a good explanation will somehow justify it for her.

One small shift I've recently made is allowing myself to pick up my kids at after-school care a little bit later in order to finish all work-related activities before they get in the car. I used to feel guilty about their long hours away from me, but studies show it's the quality, not the quantity, of time we are together that really counts.[85] But I still struggle to get through the more mundane parenting moments—like when the kids are watching TV, doing homework, or slowly eating a bowl of cereal—without picking up my phone.

———

Here is more of the feedback I received from parents in my Facebook group.

**Question: How do you try to model appropriate smartphone and social media use for your children?**

- Honestly, I suck at it and it's something I'm working on. I try not to be on my phone when my kids are awake but...it happens too often.

- We do not use our phones once home.

- I don't use the phone at the table and very rarely when I am with them. I have told my friends not to expect replies instantly to texts. I don't have Facebook or any other social media on my phone. I occasionally will use my phone to look up things, but I don't use it much when I'm with my girls. I want to make an effort to be with them, not with some little rectangle.

- We have many discussions and try to lead by example.

- Use it very little in front of them for now.

We don't need recommendations to fix this. We just need to look inward a bit more. I think our kids may surprise us and have a better handle on technology etiquette than we do. Some will have the experience of being raised by tech-distracted parents and will hopefully adjust their own styles in accordance with what they experienced.

## Lessons in Technology

The second norm that Ribble, Bailey, and Ross discussed in their article is *communication*. Our constant use of text and social media makes language arts teachers cringe. In a world where emojis are used in place of adjectives, we all have more time to practice our nonverbal communication but not in a way that will make us better communicators. The researchers don't recommend we stop using shorthand in our texts entirely, but they do recommend that teachers encourage students to use proper grammar when possible. To that end, we can also teach our kids to use plain language and keep a respectful tone when communicating online.

Ribble, Bailey, and Ross write, "Technology-infused teaching is becoming more commonplace every year. Technology in the classroom is becoming as transparent as the chalkboard and pencil. However, teaching how to use this technology has not grown accordingly. Technology-infused teaching does not always include teaching about appropriate and inappropriate uses of technology."

Giving our kids access to technology without giving them education about its proper use will inevitably hurt them. The challenge is that we are just now understanding how to best incorporate the digital world into our own lives. Our ultimate challenge is to simultaneously understand and process the culture shift taking place around us and help our children better understand the role it can healthily play in their lives.

### Giving Kids the Gear

The next thing for us to consider, suggest Ribble, Bailey, and Ross, is access. When is it the right time to give kids access to a laptop? A Nintendo Switch? An iPhone? Social media?

While there are many websites that give parents guidance, there aren't universal answers to these tough questions. In my family, we focus more on what the devices will be used for than what kind of device is being requested. For example, we had an extra laptop at home, and my second-grader was really into playing a math game online that he regularly played at school. We decided that this was a good use of technology for him and made its new home his bedroom desk. We told him that the computer was only to be used for his math game. This worked out well for about a week, and then one day I went to check on him long after he should have gone to bed. I was hearing a muffled voice and found him sitting upright at his desk watching YouTube.

Yeah, I get it. Most parents reading this might want to slap me upside the head. *Of course he'd eventually realize that the same YouTube on my iPhone was waiting for him in a separate browser window on the computer.* Kids want what they're not supposed to have. If I didn't want him on YouTube, I should have disabled it from the device.

As I prepared to write this chapter, a close friend of mine gave me a good laugh remembering how last year, her daughter made a mess of her shampoos and soaps on the shower floor. She had caught her daughter playing with them five minutes earlier and had warned her that soaps were for washing, not for playing. She closed the shower curtain and walked away.

When my friend came back to check on her daughter, the girl was still at it, this time completely covered in her twenty-dollar shampoo, and her favorite bodywash overpowered the air with its sweet scent. My friend gave her daughter a stern look. "I told you not to play with my soaps!" she said to her in utter disbelief. "Mama, I'm five," the young girl replied. "Five year-olds play with whatever is in front of them. If you didn't want me to play with it, you shouldn't have left it out."

Point taken. Lesson learned.

Kids will naturally try to push limits and access all the information and material they can. It's our job to create safe spaces, both online and offline, so that they can explore their surroundings in a way that does not put their mind or body at risk.

## Shopping Online

How much do you buy online these days? Too much? Not enough? The answer depends on context, right? No matter how many times I think I've set my Amazon "Subscribe & Save" correctly, I always end up with way too much toilet paper and not nearly enough paper towels in the storage closet to make it through the month. At the same time, I far too often find myself browsing clothing websites when I should be working because I got an email alerting me to a great sale.

When kids see us shopping online, they are seeing a combination of our efficiency at work as well as impulsivity in action. We can access more, but we also must exercise restraint. Modeling this behavior for our kids is challenging, but as parents of teens know, it is so critical.

Today's kids are targeted by companies trying to get them to buy everything from intangible things like extra skins on Fortnite to the typical tangible things we used to ask our parents to buy for us at the mall. In the middle are a vast array of subscriptions, downloads, gaming equipment, and headphone accessories. We need to be conscious of our own online impulses to better prepare our kids to participate in the online economy.

Ribble, Bailey, and Ross suggest that teachers prepare kids for commerce by engaging them "in a dialogue about using technology to purchase goods and services [and]...about good and bad experiences of purchasing goods online." Furthermore, they recommend that adults ask kids to "read comparison shopping Web sites such as CNET or AddALL to analyze comparative shopping strategies." Of course, the recommendations encourage kids to also learn about the risks of commerce online.

## Giving Kids Control While Setting Boundaries

In many middle schools, kids are gaining access to Instagram right around the same time they are beginning to learn how to use Adobe's Photoshop and Illustrator. It is also a time when they are taking pictures of themselves and of others, and distinguishing who owns what in a digital world can be confusing for adults and kids alike.

"When creating or publishing anything digitally, students have the same copyright protection as any other content creators," write Ribble, Bailey, and Ross. When we think about teaching our kids about their rights, it might be helpful to think about rights in a manner that may empower them—instead of saying, "You have no right to use that photo," maybe it's best to frame the lesson as, "That is your image, you have a right to its ownership."

These concepts fit nicely together for parents trying to practice what they preach at home. The writers encourage parents to think about the intangible safety and security risks technology poses. They mention more tangible harms, like sleeplessness and eye strain, which are some of the very real safety considerations we must look at as parents. Is your phone next to you in the bedroom? Your teen may come to expect that his should be there as well.

We need to think deeply about the security of the technology we invite into our homes as well as the technology our kids interact with throughout their day. As good digital citizens, we must feel empowered by our technology use, even though it can be overwhelming. Let your children see you read the fine print before downloading apps. Talk about online security and safety at the dinner table. You might not have the right words at first, but allow your kids the chance to see you working through the complexities of inviting technology into your life.

## Takeaways for Modeling Better Sharing Online

▶ **Look inward.** My friend Lindsay was packing the next day's lunches when she noticed her son Chris's phone pulsating on the kitchen counter. Curious to see who was texting him so late, she picked up the phone and entered the password. Like most middle school parents, Lindsay had told Chris that she would occasionally check his phone. She wasn't snooping, she told herself; she was simply doing what any concerned mother would do.[86]

What she saw was disturbing. The text was an angry message from Chris's best friend's older sister, Becky. As Lindsay looked back through Chris's messages, she saw why Becky was so upset. She opened Instagram on Chris's phone, where he had posted a picture of Becky in her bathing suit, bending over to pick something up. It wasn't a flattering image, and by the looks of the picture, Becky did not know that her photograph had been taken. The photo had garnered many comments, most of which made fun of Becky's appearance.

Chris didn't have Becky's consent to post the picture, but as Lindsay thought about what happened, she realized she hadn't done a great job teaching him consent, either. Like in many other contexts, kids learn by watching us. When I share pictures of my twelve-year-old on Facebook without checking in with him first, whether I intend for him to or not, he's getting the message that he, too, can share pictures of others without checking in. We all want our children to respect the rights of others. And one way we respect their rights is by asking for permission before sharing their image online.

While Chris may be an upstanding teen at school and super helpful at home, navigating social media may present unique challenges, and since we as parents are only just beginning to understand the ramifications of sharing online, we aren't always prepared to model by example or to teach responsible social media citizenship. While our own newness to social media may explain the lack of guidance we are giving our kids, this dearth of experience shouldn't negate our responsibilities to model ethical behavior online. We ourselves need to share responsibly. If we don't, we can't possible expect our children to.

For my first seven years on social media, I shared too much. I snapped pictures all the time. I didn't have separate friend groups and I certainly didn't ask my five-year-old to review my posts before they went live. I'm reminded of these choices daily when I review my "memories" on Facebook. Now that the information is out there, it's hard to delete it all, but there are ways to cut back. For example, lately when I review my "memories" on Facebook, I delete old posts. The data likely still exists somewhere in the cloud, but it helps me feel less overwhelmed by all the photos I've shared over the past decade.

▶ **Practice what you preach.** Children model the behavior of their parents, and when parents constantly share personal details about their children's lives and then monitor their posts for likes and followers, children take note. While most parents have their children's best interests at heart when they share personal stories on social media, there is little guidance to help them navigate parenting in the digital age.

Kids constantly absorb messages from many sources, including parents. They mimic these observed behaviors in adolescence and adulthood. It is possible that parental sharing and oversharing has taught children that sharing another person's personal pictures and stories is expected and appropriate.

Parents can help their kids better understand the implications of nonconsensual online sharing even if they've shared about their children in the past. One powerful way to do this is to offer their older children the opportunity to delete posts that cause embarrassment or shame. Before sharing any future posts about their children, parents can ask permission. This can help teens understand the power and the importance of controlling one's own digital footprint. In turn, this helps teens understand why it is critical that they, too, obtain consent before adding to, or altering, the digital footprints of others.

▶ **Teach, don't shame.** After Lindsay realized what Chris did, mother and son had a talk. While he quickly deleted the picture from his Instagram feed, much of the damage had already been done, causing hurt and embarrassment to Becky. To help Chris understand, Lindsay pulled up her own Facebook posts, many featuring photos of Chris as a very young child. She watched as he processed each picture. While there was some laughter, she could tell Chris was also surprised by many of her disclosures. They talked about the importance of controlling one's own digital footprint. To that end, Lindsay offered to delete posts that Chris found embarrassing or inappropriate. After reflecting on the conversation with his mom, Chris offered a sincere apology to Becky. He knew she still had a right to be angry, but he hoped that by taking responsibility for his actions, they could start to make amends.

———

It's not easy to find a balance between sharing our stories and teaching kids the boundaries of privacy online. Asking kids' permission feels weird—like an imbalance in the parent-child relationship. For some kids, being asked is annoying—they've already said they don't care, or in their mind they've already explained that when they look like "that" (whatever "that" means to a self-conscious preteen), they never want you to share. It's also limiting. Remember the value of sharing our stories—the power of narratives I explained in chapter three. Relying too heavily on the perspective of a six-year-old seems misplaced when we are talking about raising awareness for important social justice issues or sharing heart-pounding, heartbreaking, or heartwarming family news.

I'm only just beginning to see if (and how) my own technology blunders will one day affect my children's online sharing habits. I can only hope that my kids see I'm a work in progress, and as I learn, they too gain wisdom and become good digital citizens.

## CHAPTER EIGHT

# The Right to Be Forgotten

In some countries, the information shared about a child could be subject to deletion under a centuries-old doctrine known as "the right to be forgotten." In a nutshell, the right to be forgotten gives people the right to have information in the public sphere deleted once the information is no longer relevant to the person's reputation. Courts are reluctant to recognize a right to be forgotten in the United States because it arguably infringes on our Constitutional right to free speech.[87]

The "right to be forgotten" doctrine effectively allows individuals to change their digital footprint.[88] In a landmark ruling, based on the interpretation of the Data Privacy Directive (a European Union law), an individual filed a complaint against Google.[89] He brought his complaint because he believed that the information retrieved by Google following an internet search was not favorable or relevant to his current lifestyle—the information pertained to a debt that he had subsequently paid. The individual believed that he had a right to have the information removed from the internet, because it was harmful to his reputation. He wanted it removed from or concealed within the newspaper stories and Google searches. The court agreed, stating that the information served to "compromise the fundamental right to data protection and the dignity of persons in the broad sense, and the information would also encompass the mere wish of the person concerned that such data not be known to third parties." Google appealed; however, the appellate court agreed with the lower court. The appellate court required Google to remove the contested information from its search results, but the court did not require the newspaper to remove the information from the internet.

Would a U.S. court require Google to do the same thing for a young adult whose parent shared publicly about them when they were young? Many children now have a Google search result before they fill out their first job application. I imagine some of these kids will be embarrassed by the personal information shared publicly by their parents. They may wish the disclosures were not part of their growing digital identity. European children can ask the court to have the data removed under the right to be forgotten, but children in the United States would likely not obtain the same relief because we have strong Free Speech protections that limit the applicability of such a doctrine.

## Legal Hurdles

When parents share about life with a new baby, they benefit more than the child. The child is oblivious to the disclosure. He isn't harmed by it now. There is a chance the disclosure is even helping him a bit. His mom might be getting advice about breastfeeding, which would help him eat, or his dad might feel more supported by his online community. Parents who share online about their children are "expressing themselves." As such, they are exercising their constitutionally protected right to free speech. Most I spoke to think that's a good thing. Most people aren't so sure they want government to limit a parent's right to free speech.

Before we get into what kids might want the internet to forget, let's first take a look at what parents think the law should allow parents to share in the first place. I asked in one of my Facebook groups if there should be laws that prevent parents from oversharing online. Here is what they said:

**Question: Do you think there should be laws that prevent parents from oversharing online? If you can, please explaining the reasoning behind your answer.**

- In theory, yes, but I don't know what the law would be. Sometimes I post pics or accomplishments about my kids because our family and friends are spread out. Not sure what type of laws could/would be passed and how you would quantify "oversharing."

- No, social media platforms are private entities which we willingly enter. I think laws that prevent oversharing are a slippery slope and infringe on the rights of the person posting.

- How do you define "oversharing"? I think that would be hard to enforce and may need to be more clearly defined.

- No, I think it's a personal decision.

- No. I feel like social media is part of freedom of speech. As long as we are not sharing naked body images of our children or threatening our children, I think we can share as much as we'd like.

- No, I'm not much for restricting free will. I guess you can reason child endangerment but it's a stretch and a slippery slope.

- No. I think people should use common sense. OR maybe once your child is thirteen (age changes by state law) you can only post by proxy.

- I haven't thought this through, but my inclination is no. Obviously, I have concerns about anyone posting naked photos of their children, but I imagine existing laws would handle much of that concern. Some people are comfortable posting topless photos of their toddlers or three-year-old girls, I am just not one of them. I don't know that I would go as far as implementing a law to prevent that, either.

- Not laws. That seems extreme. Parents shouldn't post photos of their naked babies. I think that's probably against the law but if not, then that should be.

- Parents think they are just posting a "cute" photo but there are too many sick people in the world who might exploit the child without the parents ever knowing.

- I'm not sure...I have very little faith in our legal system anyway. Only if it becomes an issue of safety or sexual exploitation – i.e., sharing naked photos of an older child.

- Good question. Probably, because when the kids get older, they may be embarrassed, and it could even influence their future career and social life.

- I think there should be laws against parents posting certain content such as photos or videos of their children nude or content that could be emotionally harmful (i.e., a video of a teen being lectured about their behavior, a public post about embarrassing topics such as puberty, etc.).

- No, legislating it is not an avenue that I believe would result in anything positive.

- Yes and no. Where would one draw the line?

- I think we have enough technology nowadays that frankly the platforms themselves should be able to control some of this stuff.

- This is a fine line because I understand wanting to protect children but then where do you push the lines of parenting rights? I just feel too many laws only get followed by those who would follow guidelines anyway. And who would police the laws?

- Yes. Parents share too much without consideration to their children's privacy.

- No, parents have always been able to share, even before the internet. That's a hard line to cross.

- Yes, but I honestly have no idea where the line should be drawn.

- While it's weird and often annoying, no. Freedom of speech and all. I don't feel comfortable allowing the government to dictate parenting choices that don't involve immediate safety of children because it can become a slippery slope to loss of freedom and autonomy.

As these parents illustrate, parents in the United States value freedom of speech and parental autonomy. While parents might support the law regulating parental online speech "at the margins," broader regulations would be met with significant backlash and legal challenges. My general sense is that it is unlikely courts will afford a child relief under a doctrine like the right to be forgotten unless courts first recognize a child's right to privacy in the sharenting context. For the sake of argument, let's walk through what that would look like, and the hurdles that previous court decisions could present.

———

There are a few U.S. cases that offer us guidance on how courts may balance the competing interests of interfamily privacy. Some

of the cases are old, as a parent's right to control the upbringing of their children is part of the fabric of our nation. In 1923,
the Supreme Court was called upon to balance the interests of
both parents and the state in the context of education in *Meyer v.
Nebraska*.[90] In *Meyer*, a teacher challenged a state statute prohib-
iting the instruction of foreign languages in any school, public or
private. The U.S. Supreme Court overturned the law, holding that
the act abridged upon both the parents' and the teacher's liberty
interests. Instead of focusing on the child's right to learn the foreign language, the justices focused on the parents' right to raise
their children as they saw fit.

Two years later, in *Pierce v. Society of Sisters*,[91] the U.S. Supreme
Court addressed parental rights yet again. In that case, the justices overturned a law requiring public education for all students.
Resting its decision not on the child's liberty interest, but again
on the parents' interest, the court held that the state law that tried
to force parents to send their kids to public schools unreasonably
interfered with the parents' right to control the upbringing and
education of their children.

There are some cases that recognize that children have an
interest in privacy, but even in these cases, courts will defer to
parents in all but the most extreme circumstances. One legal case
in particular provides a strong illustration of the limits to a child's
right to privacy.[92] Charlene, a teenager, faced discipline in school
for engaging in inappropriate displays of public affection. The
school told her parents about her transgression in order to give
her a chance to challenge the school's stated punishment.

This outraged Charlene not only because she had engaged in
sexual conduct, but also because she did so with another female

student, and she had worked hard to keep her same-sex relationship hidden from her parents. The court chose to protect her parents' right to know (and to challenge the punishment if they so choose) over Charlene's right to privacy. Interestingly, the court ruled that while Charlene did have an expectation of privacy in the information, her right was outweighed by the school's need to involve her mother for Charlene's own protection.

———

In many ways, the law is about balancing interests. In the online context, it would be ideal if the law stepped in to reset the equilibrium when interests conflict. While a parent's right to share might conflict with a child's interest to privacy, the law hasn't yet stepped in to provide guidance *or* balance.

When I look back through my newsfeed, I am not attached to my earlier social media posts other than to know that I made a record of early milestones. I do like reviewing them year after year. Sometimes (rarely) I reshare them. But no one other than a handful of people are really interested in seeing my teen's first home run. His kindergarten picture is super cute, but perhaps sharing it isn't exercising my right to free speech anymore. Now it's just data, one of thousands of pictures from his youth stored in the digital cloud.

## Internet Fame

What about the parents who have turned sharing on YouTube and Instagram into the family business? There are more child celebrities today than ever before. Those kids may love it now, and perhaps they will look back favorably on their internet fame. But what if a kid grows to resent their internet stardom? When Mom and Dad are the ones putting kids on display, do kids have a right to live a private life when they get older?

Maybe not, according to the one case that looked at a version of this hypothetical through a legal lens. Oversimplified, the case stands for the proposition that once a kid is a celebrity, he is always a celebrity—even if he prefers to stay out of the spotlight later in life.

*Sidis v. FR Publishing Corp.* was decided in 1940.[93] It involved a child prodigy named William Sidis. Sidis was an accomplished kid, and his great prowess attracted lots of attention, both when he was young and also once he became an adult.

Like many kids today, Sidis's idea of a happy life was far from the life his parents may have envisioned. Unlike their apparent appreciation for fame and recognition, Sidis wanted to live a quiet, private life. He didn't like being featured in newspapers and magazines. He wanted the public to leave him alone. Much to his dismay, the *New Yorker* wouldn't oblige and ran an article that gave intimate details of his life as a reclusive guy who chose an adult life outside of the public spotlight.

Sidis sued, arguing that the *New Yorker* violated his right to privacy. The court disagreed. "William James Sidis was once a public figure," the court explained. "As a child prodigy, he excited both admiration and curiosity." The court noted he might not have appreciated the public attention at the time. But the court didn't really find his opinion relevant.

The court went on to say, "Even if Sidis had loathed public attention at that time, we think his uncommon achievements and personality would have made the attention permissible." Moreover, "Whether or not he had fulfilled his early promise, was still a matter of public concern." In essence, the court held that once someone is a public figure, they might always be considered a public figure. This might not be such a great ruling for a kid who grows up as a YouTube star but wants to spend his adulthood in peace and quiet.

## Steps Forward

This is complicated stuff. Putting the pieces together, we see that in most circumstances, kids in the United States don't have a right to privacy separate from their parents nor a right to be forgotten as the doctrine is defined under European law. But as law professor Amy Gajda explained in her article "Privacy, Press, and the Right to Be Forgotten in the United States," there are cases where courts have carved out exceptions to the First Amendment free speech right in order to delete some information from public spaces.[94] Take, for example, expungement of criminal records. While Gajda's article focuses on the need for any right to be forgotten to be grounded in presuming newsworthiness, she outlines many examples throughout American jurisprudence that suggest courts are sympathetic to privacy concerns stemming from safety, privacy, and oftentimes youth.

The first way courts could find that kids have a right to be forgotten is to carve out an exception to First Amendment free speech protections as the court has done in other contexts. The right to be forgotten could recognize that as time passes, the value of some disclosures is minimized and must make way for the competing privacy interests of the child. When a parent shares information about a child online, the expressive purpose of the disclosure diminishes as the child ages. The right to be forgotten could allow parents the freedom to talk about their children on social media and blogs. It would not infringe on parental rights to freely express his or her views on parenting, and it would allow parents to control the dissemination of information about the child as a member of the family unit. Ultimately, it supports a parent's right to free expression but also recognizes a child's right to privacy.

———

Allyson Hayes Stewart, a law professor at Charleston School of Law, has also explored these issues. "The online privacy of minors is of critical importance to most Americans," she writes in her article "Google Search Results: Buried If Not Forgotten." While children's privacy is not the focus of her article, she highlights California's children's privacy law. The law stops "websites and applications from marketing or advertising specific types of products or services to a minor, or from compiling, using or disclosing personal information of a minor." The law also requires that websites provide a way for kids to have information they post online about themselves be removed upon their request. Unlike a true right-to-be-forgotten law, this law only applies to information that the minor posts online about him- or herself. Some U.S. senators have proposed updating COPPA to include a similar eraser law provision;[95] however, like California's law, this would only allow children to delete information they post about themselves—it would not protect them from oversharing by parents.

Perhaps one could make the argument that the disclosures made by parents may start out as a form of speech, but by the time the child gets older, the information shared over the course of his or her childhood becomes not speech, but data.[96] Young adults could potentially argue that information shared by their parents may have served their parent's expressive interests long ago, but that as it accumulates over time, it becomes a form of data, like other personally identifiable information that is often protected from dissemination with laws like FERPA, HIPAA, and COPPA. While the first potential solution carves out an exception to free speech, this one instead argues that once the child is an adult, the information is no longer speech *at all*. By utilizing doctrines such as the right to be forgotten, U.S. courts could recognize that children have an evolving ability to provide consent. Under this theory, courts could hold that young children vicariously consent to parental disclosures, but as children age, they should gain more control over their personal information. Indeed, the expressive nature of the parental disclosures become data (instead of speech) as the child reaches the age of majority. This balanced-rights approach offers solutions to the conflicts that arise between children and their parents in the online world.

———

When my son searches for his name online, one of the first things that pops up is a story from our local newspaper documenting his birth. When he was younger, he thought it was neat that his picture and name made it into the local paper. These days, he couldn't care less about the article and is instead focused on creating his own online presence.

As my son does that, I expect that his own posts and achievements will take precedence on Google's search result algorithm.

That said, I am mindful that what pops up at the top of a Google search result has far less to do with newsworthiness and far more to do with the search engine optimization (SEO) work done by individual websites. While it makes more sense for Google to be populated with things my son accomplishes on his own, it's very possible that the local newspaper's SEO work will be superior to the SEO work on the websites highlighting his personal achievements. He might enter adulthood with the digital footprint I created when he was an infant.

## Key Takeaway: Laws and Conversations Must Shift to Give Kids Control of Their Digital Footprints

Today's twelve-year-old was born before Facebook became ubiquitous. Yet nine-year-olds may have had their birth announced on social media before parents called distant relatives and friends. This may not impact their lives when they get older, but the decision to allow such information to remain online—for its negative or its positive impact—should perhaps be theirs to choose. While parents hopefully share with their child's best interest at heart, it is critical that our laws and our public conversations surrounding privacy evolve to consider how our online footprints affect the youngest members of society. And we either must ensure that we have a way to protect those footprints or must accept that, through our inaction despite our growing knowledge, we are making a conscious and informed choice *not* to protect them.

## CHAPTER NINE:

# Outside Influences

Think back to the start of the school year. If your family (and your refrigerator) is anything like mine, fall means back to routines, and checklists to keep you organized.

Backpacks packed? Check.
Pantry filled with lunch snacks for the week? Check.
Extracurricular activity scheduled for the month? Check.

There are also so many forms to fill out during that back-to-school whirlwind. Most forms require little of us other than a pen, our smartphone contacts, and time—time that is usually found somewhere between pouring milk into cereal bowls and making sure everyone has (somewhat clean) socks.

Often, those forms include a sheet asking for permission to share your kids' pictures, assignments, and art online. Until your children start being able to make these choices on their own, strive to be in control of what others post online about your kids. While we may wish the law protected families from others posting about them without consent, there are gray areas.[97]

———

I asked some parents in my social media circle if anyone ever posted about their child without asking them first. I also posed a few follow-up questions. In particular, I asked if it upset them and how they handled it.

**Question: Has anyone ever posted about your child without asking you first? Did this upset you? If you were upset, how did you handle it?**

- Yes, I've had people post him who don't even know me. We might be in the same organization or have a friend in common, but we are not friends. This did upset me, and I've asked them to remove the image.

- Yes, and no, it didn't upset me. I do block out faces of kids that aren't mine [when I post] unless I can tag a parent in the post.

- Yes, and I was only mildly annoyed. If they had asked, I would have said it's OK, though, so I didn't do anything about it. It's usually just my parents.

- Yes. Yes. The only reason I was upset was because their social media was set to public. I asked them to change their privacy settings for the specific post/profile or remove the post about my child.

- Yes. I keep my Instagram private, and I had another parent with a public profile post my child with hers and tagged their school. I was upset because I don't know who her followers are, and I asked her to remove the post.

- Yes. Close friends or family but not in a way that was concerning. If someone did post about my children in a way that made me uncomfortable, I would ask them to remove it.

- Yes, my mom accidentally shared a photo of me pregnant with my second child before I had officially "announced" it on Facebook. I told her that I hadn't posted about my pregnancy. She felt horrible and took the photo down immediately.

- My dad posted when my second child was born before I did. I wasn't upset but thought it would have been nice if he waited or asked. But I know he was so excited, so I was fine with it.

- My husband and my mother-in-law have on rare occasion. My husband and I talked and he changed or removed posts. He talked to my mother-in-law and she removed the post and has been much more cautious in posting since then.

- Occasionally my in-laws do, and it is often an issue. For example, they posted about my gender reveal before I did, and I wanted to be the first to share the news. Sometimes they post things that embarrass me personally—like a cute photo of my son with my horribly messy kitchen in the background. Sometimes I ask

them not to and explain why, other times I let it slide. I pick my
battles with them.

- Yes, we were previously non-sharers and my mom posted a few
  pics on Facebook and we were not happy and asked her to take
  them down. Later we decided that Facebook was OK for kid pics
  because of family so far away and it felt too complicated to try
  to control the flow of pictures.

- Yes, a friend posted a picture of our daughter. We were mad.
  Hubby yelled at her. Another acquaintance posted a picture of
  our daughter and was told to take it down immediately.

- Yes. My mother-in-law had a habit of taking photos of my
  children from my profile and sharing them herself. It upset me
  because she has a lot of complete strangers on her friends list.
  I actually ended up blocking her from my profile to put an end
  to it.

- Yes. An extended family member commented about my first
  pregnancy on my wall, even though we hadn't announced to
  everyone. I deleted and messaged her to explain why.

My unscientific poll suggests that parents have had experiences where other people shared pictures of their kids without asking
first, and while they've been frustrated, many were able to work it
out without too much conflict. Of course, my circle of participants
was small and involved parents who are *on* social media. Parents

who choose not to go online or go online rarely would likely have much stronger reactions.

## Rights versus Interests

Last April, parents were outraged after a day care posted a video of their toddler's horrified reaction to the Easter bunny. While many people, including Jimmy Kimmel, shared the video thinking it was adorable, the family never gave permission for the child's image to be shared.[98] Even if they had permitted some images, should the school have had the right to share *this one* without asking first?

Every few months, a concerned parent reaches out to me because someone shared a picture of his or her child on social media without asking first. The concerned parent is rightly upset, and usually approaches me to help them identify a legal remedy to the problem. Unfortunately, I often don't have a legal argument ready to go. This area of the law is nuanced, and generally speaking, one does not have a legal claim against another for sharing pictures online.

We often think about privacy as a right, like our right to free speech or our right to bear arms. But unlike those rights, which are expressly stated in the U.S. Constitution, the right to privacy is less clear. Eleven state constitutions *do* include a right to privacy;[99] however, even in these states, there are limits to how this right applies in practice. There are many Supreme Court cases that infer a right to privacy under federal law,[100] but again, like the state laws mentioned above, this right has limits that will often preclude parents from asserting the right on behalf of their children when images are shared online.

## Is it Private or Public?

Examples of these privacy limits abound. Let's start with the *Howell* case, a New York case involving the publication of a psychiatric patient's picture in the *New York Post*.[101] In *Howell*, the plaintiff was receiving treatment at an inpatient psychiatric facility. A photojournalist took a photograph of the plaintiff as she walked around with another patient on the outdoor grounds.

The woman walking alongside the plaintiff was Hedda Nussbaum, someone of great public interest. One of her children, Lisa, had died due to child abuse. The *New York Post* published the photograph of Nussbaum and the plaintiff next to a picture of Nussbaum on the date of her arrest. (The charges were later dismissed.[102]) As the court explained, "In the earlier photograph, Nussbaum's face is bruised and disfigured, her lips split and swollen, and her matted hair is covered with a scarf. By contrast, in the photograph taken at Four Winds, Nussbaum's facial wounds have visibly healed, her hair is coiffed, and she is neatly dressed in jeans, a sweater and earrings. Plaintiff, walking alongside her, smiling, is in tennis attire and sneakers. The caption reads: 'The battered face above belongs to the Hedda Nussbaum people remember—the former live-in lover of accused child-killer, Joel Steinberg. The serene woman in jeans at left is the same Hedda, strolling with a companion in the grounds of the upstate psychiatric center where her face and mind are healing from the terrible wounds Steinberg inflicted.'"

The court ruled that while individuals in New York state had a codified right to privacy, that right did not extend to the facts of this case. While the plaintiff might have wanted to keep the facts of her psychiatric condition private, the newsworthiness of Nussbaum's recovery was of public interest, and therefore, the *Post* was within its right to publish the photograph.

## Data Collection in Schools

Many schools use websites and apps to help kids learn, behave, and participate in classroom activities.[103] My kids (and apparently their teachers) love these online tools, but the collection and use of my kids' personal information concerns me. Ultimately, it seems that schools engage in classroom activities and kid surveillance to try to help individual kids learn and help educational systems work better. In their paper "The Datafied Child: The Dataveillance of Children and Implications for Their Rights," professors Lupton (whose work we discussed in chapter two) and Ben Williamson (a Chancellor's Fellow at the University of Edinburgh) write, "Children are monitored not only by commercial companies when they log into software, but also their personal health, wellbeing and education details are tracked by government agencies from early infancy until they start work. The idea is to use these big datasets to contribute to educational policy."[104] In the past, personalization referred to programs that were individualized to the particular student's needs, but now this same term is used to describe how commercial companies use data to personalize student learning. It's unclear, explain the researchers, what this will mean for children and their rights. "New kinds of children's rights instruments that might combine with and mitigate the potential risks and harms of data surveillance assemblages involving children remain an urgent priority for policy development," write Lupton and Williamson.

While governments create many of the online networks that track childhood success (and failure) in school, governments (through their publicly funded schools) also contract with private companies to track student progress. ClassDojo, an app my middle child used in kindergarten, is one example of such a private company. I was able to download the app onto my phone and see in real time how my son was progressing during the day. When his color changed on the behavior chart, I was able to get an update instantaneously. In the United Kingdom, 70 percent of schools use the app, and in the United States, the percentage of schools using the app is reportedly as high as 95 percent.[105]

As is true for most apps, I see pros and cons to this sort of monitoring. Let's stick with ClassDojo and talk through what we know, and what we don't know, about this common classroom monitoring app.

▶ The things I like:

    ▷    The media hasn't reported on any widespread privacy violations regarding ClassDojo, and it's been around for quite a while. Could a breach happen? Sure. Has it happened? Not that I know of. The ClassDojo website makes clear that the company won't sell "personal information to anyone for any purpose." It's important to note that many other school-based apps do not have such pro-child language.

    ▷    ClassDojo prides itself on not creating a permanent record on children. It claims to delete information after one year. Parents can request deletion earlier if they so choose.

▷ The website reports that its feedback is over 90 percent positive. Parents and teachers think ClassDojo improves learning outcomes and behavior.

► The things I still wonder about:

▷ Some parents are concerned that teachers can't fully consent to children's use of ClassDojo, and that is what often happens—teachers, not parents, sign up their students and start entering data.

▷ Even if the data isn't shared outside of the school, some parents are concerned that it could potentially label a child based on his behaviors. Tony Portfield, a software engineer speaking with the New York Times, suggested, "It's a little early to be doing that to my six-year-old."[106]

▷ Some teachers who use ClassDojo share the information publicly with the class. While this could help with behavior modification, it can also hurt kids by embarrassing them or harming their reputation.

It is important to recognize that ClassDojo is one app of many, and it has a strong following because it claims to have benefits for teachers, parents, and students. Like many aspects of parenting and sharing online, it's perfectly OK to have mixed feelings about apps' use in school and family life. As with all technology, parents must think about what privacy risks the new opportunities present alongside their benefits. It isn't as simple as saying, "No, we won't use any apps that could compromise our privacy," because technology is embedded into just about everything we do.

———

Attorney and privacy consultant Brad Shear has observed the effects of cumulative data collection on students.[107] He is advocating for a "National Student Data Deletion Day." Under his plan, all public schools K–12 would delete students' browsing history, student work, and behavioral information saved on third-party platforms. They would also delete any information pertaining to the physical location of students or biometric data retrieved from student accounts, like their meal plans.[108] Shear is a privacy advocate and a concerned parent, and he's thought hard about ways we can embrace technology while protecting our kids from the growing concerns that data collection presents. "I have come to the realization that more needs to be done to raise awareness about these issues and to effectuate change," Shear explains.

## Takeaways for Taking Charge of What *Others* Share Online about *Your* Kids

Even without the benefit of comprehensive privacy laws, there are a few steps we can take to protect our children's personal information when third parties want to share it.

▶  **Tell friends and family about your privacy wishes.** Most of the people in our lives won't intrude on our digital footprints maliciously. Instead, most do so because they *themselves* have not yet considered its importance.

► **Be sure your social media settings require you to approve posts when you've been tagged.** This way, in many instances, you can be the first to see when your image or your child's image is being shared online.

► **Set up Google alerts to let you know if your name or your child's name is included in anything published online.** This free and easy service will alert you any time the name is shared in a news article or public social media post. Google isn't the only service that does this. Talkwalker and Mention are two other platforms with similar offerings.

► **When signing up kids for school or extracurricular events, let the school know of your sharing preferences, and ask if they have a policy in place that protects your wishes.** If the school does not have a policy, offer to help create one. Other parents who haven't read this book or thought through the issue will thank you!

► **Research the web-based systems your child's school uses in the classroom.** Insist that the school share information about these programs with all parents and ask for a meeting with not only the school, but also the third-party provider if you have questions. Don't assume the school will protect your child's privacy. Like many of us, administrators and teachers are only beginning to understand how to best use technology in their lives *and* in the classroom.

► **When someone does share your child's image without**

**asking first, consider if it was done to cause harm or was done out of ignorance.** If it was ignorance, use it as a learning opportunity for the other person. Share why you are concerned. Instead of assuming your input won't change their actions in the future, consider that they hadn't even considered the issue, and that they might appreciate your perspective.

As our kids grow up on our newsfeeds, so too are we growing up as adults through social media's ever-present lens. We are all new to this—parents, school administrators, coaches, religious leaders, everyone. There are no clear guidelines to guide our decision-making process as we share on social media, but there *is* one clear message all adults should heed: When it comes to sharing about children on social media, parents (and when developmentally appropriate, older children) should be the ones giving the OK, and parents must be the ones setting the boundaries.

## CHAPTER TEN

# Kids, Tweens, and Teens Online

There has been a major culture shift in our online sharing culture, and parents play only one part of this groundswell. The privacy issues discussed in earlier chapters aren't only concerns when parents and other caring adults in a child's life share, but they are also apparent when kids share about themselves. As parents, we can only hope that our careful sharing practices lead our kids to follow suit. In order to practice what we preach, we need to be authentic and thoughtful when we talk to our kids about healthy online habits.

In my work with young people, I am constantly reminded of how quickly a tween's casual remark online can result in catastrophic misunderstandings. I also often see how quickly a relatively well-behaved teen can go from responsible in the real world to reprehensible in the virtual one. Something about online spaces cause tweens to quickly forget the golden rule. Perhaps "do unto others as you'd have others do unto you" is easier to understand when we stand face-to-face with others. But our actions online can have devastating consequences.

## Staying Out of Trouble

In most states, cyberbullying is a crime. Kids who cyberbully classmates will often face school discipline, but many will also find themselves meeting with law enforcement and possibly finding themselves in delinquency court as well. Threats that might seem harmless face-to-face can result in a stay at a juvenile detention center and possibly even a long-term program. As parents who had little more than a pager when we were in school, it's challenging to relate to kids who are trying to navigate social media and texting while their frontal cortex is still being developed.

We've all seen the ramifications of inappropriate teen sharing in the news. A child sent a partially nude picture of herself to a high school boyfriend, resulting in a child pornography charge—for both minors. Another took a video of a friend doing something embarrassing and posted it on Instagram, resulting in his parents and school being put on high alert that legal action could be taken. As a parent, each time I hear about or work with someone facing such adult consequences for immature actions, I nag my own teen, reminding him that a moment of posting can cause a lifetime of consequence.

## Protection versus Privacy

Despite this awareness, I struggle to balance the need to protect my kids from their own youth with the need to give them some semblance of privacy regarding their relationships. When I was a tween and young teen, I often said or did the wrong things in my social circles. I was embarrassed by my own actions, and while my parents caught some of my misdeeds, many went unseen. I learned from my mistakes because of their natural consequences— lost friendships, lost trust, changes in my relationships that I didn't want. If my parents saw all my mistakes, I'd probably have learned the lesson—but I'd also have had to deal with the shame that would inevitably come along with it.

———

There are two kinds of shame applicable when it comes to social media and our teenagers. The first one is more public—and it focuses on how some parents use social media to shame their kids. Sue Scheff, a leading social media expert and author of *Shame Nation: The Global Epidemic of Online Hate*, writes about a parent who shamed a teenager on social media in an attempt to call her daughter out for claiming to be nineteen and posting inappropriate pictures on social media.[109] "On one hand, it's hard not to admire this mom's determination to protect her child and prevent her from growing up before she's ready," Scheff writes. But "it's also hard not to wonder about the potential fallout between the parent and child," Scheff wisely warns. Her book highlights the often overlooked consequences of shaming others on social media, and it encourages us all to look deeper into how we can protect ourselves and be in control of our online lives.

Teens can also experience shame when their parents monitor social media, particularly when the teen acts in a way that disappoints Mom or Dad. In many families, this sort of shame is more difficult to navigate. While a bit of shame can help kids become more empathetic and responsible adults, it can also have negative implications. In their article "Shame and Guilt-Proneness in Adolescents: Gene-Environment Interactions," authors Aurora Szentágotai-Tătar, Adina Chiş, Romana Vulturar, Anca Dobrean, Diana Mirela Cândea, and Andrei C. Miu explain that over the long run, shame isn't a good thing. "Studies have consistently linked shame-proneness in children and adolescents with anxiety, depression, eating disorders, externalizing symptoms and delinquent behavior."[110]

As a parent, I am concerned that if I look closely at my child's online keystrokes, I will inevitably witness behavior that I will feel a need to correct. Finding the balance between empathetically correcting and inadvertently shaming him is challenging. Unlike my own experiences offline, I don't have memories of coming of age alongside an iPhone to help guide me.

## Teens Want Privacy

As we discuss privacy online, it is helpful to once again think about privacy rights of children in general—those that both bind them to and separate them from their parents. In their article "Privacy for Children," Benjamin Shmueli and Ayelet Blecher-Prigat explore how the law views a child's right to privacy not in relation to third parties, but instead as it relates to their parents.[111] "Children need physical privacy in order to develop their individuality, their independence and their self-reliance, as well as for the sake of their creativity and other attributes important to personal development," the authors write. They go on to explain that children don't only need privacy, but they also need to be able to have some control with who they interact with, and how they do it.

Shmueli and Blecher-Prigat explain that this need also includes "information management," which they define as "choosing when to disclose information to others." As children get older, the need to make these choices only increases, and a parent's role in controlling information must make way for a teen's competing interest in controlling her own digital footprint. This may include what information parents share about the teen, as well as information the teen herself wishes to share.

———

Like many of his peers, my middle schooler is starting to explore social media. We started with Instagram. I'm not recommending it over other social media sites. They all have significant drawbacks. They all present opportunities for bullying, poor judgment calls, oversharing, creating a negative self-image, and distorting normal teen conversations in ways never imaginable when I was growing up.

But as I said in the first chapter of this book, a culture shift has taken place. Just as the baby book has been replaced by the Facebook newsfeed, old-school phone calls and note-passing have been replaced in many teen social circles by Snaps and private messages (that are probably not actually very private). It's hard to socialize without access to the same communication tools friends are using.

As my son "got acquainted" with social media, I choose not only to follow him, but also to log in *as him* because I know how quickly digital footsteps can traverse troublesome paths. As a mom to a new tween, I wondered, *Am I intruding on his privacy by doing so?*

## Find a Balance

I've often turned to professors Shmueli and Blecher-Prigat to help me find a balance between my need to supervise my children and their need for autonomy. Their work suggests that it is difficult to balance the competing interests of protecting children and honoring their privacy. "How children's privacy should be weighed and balanced against other interests—whether the interests of the child herself, a parent, the family, or social interests—should be determined in each specific context," they explain.

Interestingly, they note that while common sense tells us that as children get older, their need for privacy increases, so too does their need for protection (as the "risks entailed by privacy are much higher for youth than for younger children"). The professors note that, while a parent's responsibility to protect his or her children is paramount, it is also important not to invade their privacy when doing so wouldn't "advance the child's safety."

When my teen engages online, I am often quick to judge (and lecture) about his choices of pictures to share and comments to make. I'm a recovering helicopter parent, and my incessant supervision doesn't sit well with a teenage boy coming into his own. As much as I want to control his digital footprint, research reminds me that I need to let go sometimes, and like the professors explained in their article, allow him an opportunity to create his own relationships and navigate how he shares information about himself. It is all part of the process of growing up.

In her book *The Art of Screen Time*, Anya Kamenetz points out that under our legal system, ordinary citizens can't be wiretapped without the government first getting a search warrant.[112] Kamenetz, an author and the lead education correspondent for NPR (National Public Radio), writes, "The warrant expires and must be renewed after a period of time." She continues, "We probably should apply some similar, if not more generous, standard of liberty at home. Placing your kids on digital house arrest without prior justification is a recipe for evasion and rebellion." Kamenetz asks a great follow-up question: "If we demand that kind of compliance in our homes, what message are we sending?"

Her message resonated with me. I spend my workdays protecting children's rights from third-party actors. At home, I have a different role to play as my children's caregiver and protector, but I want to balance my need to control with their need for autonomy. Kamenetz doesn't advocate for parents to shun supervision—quite the opposite, in fact. Instead, she encourages parents to allow their children screen time as well as offer them guidance and support. "Fostering both autonomy and connectedness has never been more important," Kamenetz writes.[113]

## Teens on Social Media

I asked my group of parents when they thought kids should begin accessing social media. Here are some of their answers.

Question: When do you think children should first get their own social media accounts? Should parents monitor their accounts? If so, at what age should parents stop monitoring their accounts?

- Middle school—if the child can emotionally handle it. And with constant parental monitoring. As long as under eighteen, my children know I will pick up their phone at any time and look at their posts.

- This is a tough one, because I'm so far from it. I would say at some point in the teen years, and parents should fully monitor it until they move out of the parents' home.

- My kids got Instagram in seventh grade with lots of parent interaction. I still monitor my kids, rising freshman and senior. But I will not when they leave for college. Lots of good talking points have come from me watching their accounts. They know I am watching.

- I don't think they should get social media until high school. I do think parents should monitor the accounts and that they should stop after high school graduation

- Sixteen. They should be monitored until they graduate high school.

- When they ask for one, I think talking to them about the responsibility is important. I think they should be monitored at first but keep asking the child if they're OK with it. Being open and honest is best.

- Personally, anything before fifteen is too young in my eyes. Definitely monitor! Kiddos can be way too naive. I'll stop monitoring my kiddo's account at eighteen.

- Thirteen and monitor as long as you feel they may need guidance.

- High school, yes to monitoring, never stop! Haha, maybe eighteen since they are technically adults.

- Given the age of my children, I haven't thought this through, but my husband and I are definitely of the mindset to wait as late as possible regarding smartphones and social media. I have major concerns about children's inability to escape bullying nowadays.

- I think high school age (13/14) is acceptable and absolutely parents should monitor all of their accounts and set ground rules that their kids cannot create an account without permission. At eighteen is when I'll stop monitoring their accounts...maybe.

- Teenagers seem like an OK age to get an account. Thirteen or fourteen maybe. I will monitor their accounts, until maybe seventeen or eighteen? I think that all depends on the child and the parents?

- Right now, I have a preteen and am seriously considering not 'til they are eighteen.

- Around sixteen. Legal adult age isn't until eighteen so they should monitor until then.

- When they are mature enough to handle it. Yes, please, parents should monitor until they are eighteen.

- I would prefer my children not use social media until they are responsible enough to do so without being monitored.

- Fourteen—parents should ALWAYS monitor until the age of eighteen.

- Teen. Absolutely 100 percent! Until eighteen?

- Oh boy...I haven't put a lot of thought since my oldest is only five. But in the back of my head I want to put it off for as long as possible.

- Ideally, high school. I worked with middle schoolers for several years. The amount of problems social media caused and the various poor choices facilitated by social media were astonishing. If we allow it before then, it will be closely monitored and used only in common areas of the house.

- I would say not before middle school and that should be on a "juvenile" account where parental authorization is required for messages and posts.

These parents had some great ideas and feel firmly that while social media is OK for teens, parents also need to monitor their usage. Constant monitoring requires a new level of parental supervision that our parents and grandparents never had to contend with...but it seems all but required in order to protect our kids *from themselves* on social media and beyond.

## What Kids Need to Stay Safe Online

The World Health Organization "developed a framework that examines key dimensions of parenting or parental roles that positively affect adolescent well-being: connection, behaviour control, respect for individuality, modelling appropriate behaviour, and provision and protection."[114] As part of that development, Sonia Livingstone and Jasmina Byrne explored how these dimensions apply to the online interactions families face in their book chapter, "Parenting in the Digital Age: The Challenges of Parental Responsibility in Comparative Perspective." The researchers recognize that even in adolescence, children need appropriate limits (behavior control), yet while setting those limits, parents must respect their children's individuality in both live and digital spaces. Perhaps most relevant to the sharenting debate, Livingstone and Byrne discuss the role of modeling appropriate behavior. The researchers highlight the need for parents to recognize that they alone will be unable to meet all of their child's needs for guidance online, and as such, they encourage parents to value the roles of teachers, peers, and other potential influencers in their teen's life, with the goal of helping to provide children with the protection they need in an ever-changing digital world.

Some state laws in the United States are better than others when it comes to protecting teens online. Writing for the *New York Times*, Somini Sengupta explained that California is often a "vanguard when it comes to digital privacy."[115] In her article "Sharing, with a Safety Net," Sengupta wrote about California's children's privacy law before it was enacted, highlighting that the state was generally more responsive to protecting its citizens online than other states.[116] She quotes James Steyer, the chief executive officer of Common Sense Media, as saying, "Kids and teenagers often self-reveal before they self-reflect." As someone who represents kids in court and tries to guide my own kids at home, this statement hit home for me. Unlike things I said as a teen that could be quickly forgotten, the things today's teens say could remain with them throughout their lives, haunting them for years to come.

———

As law slowly catches up to technology, I am hopeful we will see more states (and perhaps our federal government) do a better job protecting kids from the actions of others online, and that they recognize the developmental realities of adolescence. It would be great if the laws provided teens with tools to better manage their own digital identities in a world that is becoming more and more defined not by our offline actions, but by our online words.

Like COPPA, many of the laws that pertain to children's data collection don't apply to kids once they reach thirteen or fourteen. This is unfortunate, because the younger years aren't only the time when kids are carving out their own online identities. Lawmakers need to consider the well-being of not just grade school kids, but teenagers as well. Expanded legislation could really help protect them, both in what they share and what others continue to share about them as they get older.

## Shortcomings in the Law

As kids use online platforms, third parties can access, store, and sell their information. This creates many ethical concerns. While COPPA is intended to protect children's data from being collected without parental consent, it only protects children under age thirteen. The implications of this reality are frightening. Additionally, even when COPPA applies, privacy violators often only come to the attention of parents and concerned child advocates *after* they infringe on children's personal information.

Consider the app TikTok (formerly called Musical.ly).[117] I saw it gain popularity in my own community about two years ago, when my son and his friends wanted to use the app to record themselves singing popular songs and then sharing with their friends. When the app was popular with my kiddo, many of TikTok's users were under thirteen, and the app was collecting data (names, email addresses, etc.) from its users. The FTC, finding that TikTok knew the users were under thirteen but collected information anyway, stepped in and TikTok entered into a major settlement to resolve the case.

According to an article on Vox, the current version of the app says kids under age thirteen aren't allowed to use it.[118] But many are still concerned that young kids are able to sign up for an account. This can be especially dangerous because there are private messaging features built into the app, and predators can use these features to reach out directly to kids.

A CNET.com article written by Shelby Brown explored this risk and quoted a spokesperson for the National Society for the Prevention of Cruelty to Children, reporting, "We know that a significant amount of children are being contacted via popular livestreaming apps, such as TikTok, by abusers who are using them as a hunting ground."[119] I visited TikTok's website, which did have a safety section for parents.[120] In it, TikTok reminded parents that its platform was designed for kids over age thirteen and offered parents guidance on what to do if they found their younger children using it. The website also provided guidance and links for concerned parents on subjects such as bullying, online safety, and even suicide. It might be nice that the app has guidelines, but in order for them to work, they need to be enforced.

There are hundreds, if not thousands, of apps that are not appropriate for kids but are still easily obtained by them. The legal system is not well-prepared to protect kids from risks posed by these apps. We need better laws to protect children online, and we need to hold companies accountable when they invade upon a child's privacy.

In my work with teenagers, I've become overly familiar with how kids can harm themselves online. A teenager's brain is not fully developed. Slow brain development plus lasting digital footprints is a recipe for disaster, and social media provides a land mine rich in opportunity for kids to get into trouble.

COPPA provides kids with some protections, but it does nothing to protect teens as they begin to interact on social media. Caitlin Costello, Dale McNiel, and Renée Binder explain in their article "Adolescents and Social Media: Privacy, Brain Development, and the Law" that "Even if COPPA were perfectly enforced and effective in protecting the privacy of children under age 13, youths aged 13 to 17 are not protected by the law. The FTC has said that although COPPA does not apply to those aged 13 to 17, 'the FTC is concerned about teen privacy and does believe that strong, more flexible, protections may be appropriate for this age group.'"[121] The authors highlight that there are many things teens *want* to be able to do, but the law rightly limits their actions in many ways. While laws limit kids, they protect them far less often.

## The Teenage Brain

Next, let's think about teenage decision-making. As Costello, McNiel, and Binder explain, "Adolescents have generally reached analytic maturity by their mid-teens, [but] their still-developing experiential systems are particularly susceptible to social and emotional factors (e.g., peer pressure, romantic attachment), and their capacity for behavioral self-regulation is incomplete. Neuroscience research has shown adolescent brains to be in a continuous state of maturation, demonstrating changes in myelination, synaptic pruning, and development of the prefrontal cortex that occur into the mid 20s."

When we give teens access to social media early, we are giving them independence. But at the same time, we are giving them access to a world in which they may not be ready to fully function in. Parents are correct in being slow to let go of control when giving teens unfettered online access. While COPPA suggests that kids over thirteen are ready to fully participate in online activities, brain science says otherwise. Unless and until the law steps in to offer teens more protection in digital spaces, parents need to be well-informed consumers, gatekeepers, and advocates to protect their teens online.

## Introduce Digital Spaces Slowly

While it might be great to "wait until eighth [grade]"[122] to give a child a smartphone, it is important to talk with kids about social media interactions and texting etiquette long before middle school.

Kids as young as four already understand that they exist separately from their parent.[123] Little kids can build friendships and can already compare themselves to others. In these early years of self-expression, we can encourage kids to interact with their family and friends over FaceTime. We can give them a (well-protected) old iPhone and let them take pictures of their day. When our kids begin to read and write, we can encourage them, under our supervision, to send text messages to family members. When we post pictures of them online, we can read our young children the comments, and we can let our children respond to caring family members and friends. These little steps help slowly prepare them for the inevitable online world in which they will find themselves in as they get closer to adolescence.

Without this slow introduction, kids can become quickly overwhelmed with the opportunities—both good and bad—that their smartphone offers. It might sound great to keep a child off social media until eighth grade, but if he suddenly gets five social media accounts on his thirteenth birthday, he might get himself into serious trouble. Instead, parents can introduce kids to the concept of online communities early on, thereby taking away some of the mystique and possibly helping their child develop a healthier relationship with virtual spaces.

## Annie's Way

My friend Annie is a bit older than me. She rarely shares on social media. Not sharing about her kids comes easily to Annie. She's a pretty private person. "Sharing takes a lot of work, and as a result, it's not something I like to do," Annie explained to me. "In fact, when we are out and about, sometimes I have to stop myself and think, *Gee, I should take a picture of it.* I guess I tend to live in the moment more."

While her phone is rarely out for memory-making, her daughters use technology differently. Recently, while the family was on vacation, her two daughters were taking pictures nonstop. "At one point, I had to say, 'Phones down, no more pictures. Let's just enjoy what we are looking at. Let's just enjoy right now.'"

I am inspired by how easily Annie can shut off the enticement of sharing online. She attributes it to a few factors. "Some people like the pat on the back they get when they post on social media. I don't care about that. I know many of the people on my social media feed, but some of the people in the feed wouldn't know me if they saw me in a room. It just doesn't matter to me what they think." Annie also explained that posting on social media seems to take effort. "When I want to post something, I have to think very hard about what to post about. If I posted more often, I would have to make an effort to pull the phone out and take pictures."

Despite her reluctance to share, her older daughter shares

frequently online. Annie remembers a time when her daughter was in middle school and didn't have a phone. She found that her daughter needed her own phone to have a social life. "I would say to her, 'We have a house phone, your friends can call you on it.' But the reality is that kids don't call much anymore, they text or Snapchat. If I wanted her to make friends and do things, she had to have an online presence."

Annie allows her older daughter to have an iPhone (she gave it to her in middle school), but she feels parents need to set limits and monitor their teen's tech use. "I recommend parents hold off as long as possible," she told me. "Most of the time, their brains are not mature enough to limit themselves, so parents need to step in." Annie recommends that parents find ways to encourage their kids to interact offline. In her house, she often collects the phones when friends come over. She's considering putting a basket at the front door. "There were times where they'd be sitting next to each other laughing, and I would realize they were texting back and forth, even though they could easily just talk face-to-face!"

Reflecting on her own preferences to interact in person, Annie highlighted that "as much as kids think they are involved with so many people because they touch base with so many friends in a single day, I think they might actually be a lot more isolated than I ever was as a teen. If they are not constantly interacting, they feel alone." This is why Annie makes it a priority to pull her kids away from technology. She sends them to sleepaway camp every summer. She (usually) doesn't allow phones at the dinner table. "I think it's just better to live in the moment," Annie explained. "I like to engage with people directly. I prefer an in-person meeting or phone call to a text anytime." While she knows her kids might not make the same technology decisions she's made, Annie wants to give them the tools to know how to be content without the technology, even if they choose to engage with it routinely as they get older.

## John's Way

John's son, Mark, is responsible, resourceful, and most of all, trustworthy. John was able to leave Mark home with younger siblings by the time he was twelve, and he empowered his son to prepare his own lunches and do his own laundry at an even earlier age. When it came time to give Mark a cell phone, John approached it differently than Annie. He didn't hesitate to hand one over. John knew Mark would approach his digital device—and the online world it opened up—in the same manner he'd approached everything else.

Mark is now heading off to NYU in the fall. As John looks back on his son's adolescence, he is proud of himself for trusting his gut. The pair spoke openly about his online experiences as they occurred, and as far as he knows, the only trouble he ever got into online was when he didn't report someone else who was bullying a friend in an online chat. Mark realized his mistake days later, bringing the issue to his father's attention so that he could help him problem solve and get his friend help. But John knows his experience with Mark is somewhat unique, and that most kids do struggle to stay out of trouble online. His second son, Liam, is approaching adolescence. John questions whether the same strategy (no monitoring, only talking) will work for him as well.

Many parents don't ever unlock their child's smartphone, let alone review their child's social media account. While some of these parents do so out of ignorance (and those are probably not the ones reading this book!), others do so out of a strong respect for their child's privacy, and a belief that any actual monitoring, however minimal, intrudes inappropriately on their child's personal space. Most look to handle these issues on a case-by-case basis, depending on the developmental abilities of their children. This is the approach John took with Mark, and it is how he will navigate these same issues with his younger son, Liam.

This option isn't for every family. Most kids will need a higher level of supervision, especially during the early teenage years. To use this option effectively, parents need to first understand what's at stake when handing their child access to the online world. John had this confidence, led less by his understanding of online platforms and more by his understanding of his son's level of maturity and abilities. Not a helicopter parent by any means, he wanted his son to feel empowered. He also believed that Mark needed to be responsible, on his own, for his own actions and misdeeds. John's open communication pattern allowed for him to do so in a way that made monitoring the smartphone and apps unnecessary. And Mark's honesty and resourcefulness allowed him to correct his own mistakes when they arose.

## Cheryl's Way

Cheryl talks to her kids about social media *a lot*. A child psychologist, Cheryl knows the importance of modeling good online behavior, and how crucial it is that parents talk to their kids about online interactions that *could* happen before they *do* happen. Unlike John, she sees her role as more than an instructor. Cheryl monitors her daughter, Kylee, very carefully online.

There are apps available to help parents keep tabs on their children's online activity. The Bark app alerts parents when concerning key words make their way across a child's device, sending parents instant notifications of talk about suicide, drugs, and pornography.[124] The OurPact app lets parents set schedules, limiting apps available at certain hours and even giving parents the ability to turn their child's phone on and off remotely.[125] The iPhone has a built-in parental control center that allows parents to set age restrictions on music and videos and prevent kids from downloading new apps or making in-app purchases without parental approval.

Despite the best apps, parents who want to truly monitor their children's phones must be prepared to pick up the phones and look carefully at the texts and photos inside. Cheryl created a contract with her daughter, requiring her to let Cheryl know her passwords and promising not to delete pictures and texts without talking with her first. Cheryl knows that despite her word, she still can do so, and she's found that reviewing her daughter's iCloud backup, which saves even deleted items, gives her the best idea of what her daughter is doing online, which guides their conversations offline as well.

---

Of course, there are a multitude of options when it comes to introducing digital spaces to tweens and teens. Annie, Mark, and Cheryl all approached it a bit differently, and each had their own reasons for choosing the path they took. And even with monitoring, all agree that giving children access to the internet requires more than the right apps—it requires a little bit of trust, and a lot of faith. Kids will make mistakes, and well-informed parents are best suited to help them navigate back to safety on social media.

Some uniquely situated kids, like young athletes, might ask for social media accounts earlier than other kids their own age. Lynn, one mother I spoke to, realized that her daughter would benefit from having a social media account to stay connected with her competition and camp friends across the country. At first, it seemed like a safe option, as her daughter was protective of her privacy without much parental involvement. But Lynn became concerned about other children—and at times, other parents—using social media to bully her daughter, and aware of the pressures young competitors face to promote brands online. In the end, many parents of athletes explained to me, it's all about balance. Kids, especially those who are active and independent offline, need the opportunity to explore virtual spaces on their own, but parents also need to be aware of what their kids might encounter.

## Create a Plan

The American Academy of Pediatrics (AAP) recommends that families create a "Family Media Use Plan" to help guide parents and children toward responsible media use. As explained on their website, "Media should work for you and within your family values and parenting style. When used thoughtfully and appropriately, media can enhance daily life. But when used inappropriately or without thought, media can displace many important activities such as face-to-face interaction, family-time, outdoor-play, exercise, unplugged downtime and sleep."[126]

While it can be time-consuming, creating a media use plan is a great first step toward helping your kids (and yourself) think about how social media affects our families, and it can open the door to important conversations about keeping kids safe online. Parents can create an interactive plan on the AAP website.[127] Some of the issues addressed by the plan include:

▸ **Plan *where* screens will be used.** Are phones permitted at the kitchen table? In the bedroom? While doing homework?

▸ **Plan *when* screens will be used.** I know a long car trip is a great time to catch up with our kids, but I often want to use it as a time to catch up with my Facebook newsfeed. Exploring this question with our kids requires us to also consider how we will model the behavior. Admittedly, I am terrible at this. This means I need to either change the rules or, better yet, change my behavior.

▸ **Plan *how* screens will be used.** It's important to set some general guidelines about how the family will use media. Do we use social media individually? Do we share accounts? If a child/teen has access to social media, will parents be checking it regularly? Will we allow our kids some say over what we post on our own social media feeds?

▸ **Practice kindness.** Our kids get lots of practice (and instruction) on being kind to one another in our brick-and-mortar world. They also need practice being kind online. And while (hopefully) they won't be interacting much on social media until they are teens, there are many ways kids can practice digital citizenship throughout elementary and middle school.

We can model this concept through our own online interactions, and we can invite kids to watch (or do) it with us. We can encourage them to respond to family members who like their pictures. We can review chat threads on their online academic platforms. We can teach them about the longevity of a digital footprint. And we can share with them examples of digital interactions that help us and digital interactions that hurt us.

▶ **Be open to the benefits.** While there are caveats, the AAP advice recognizes that "online relationships are part of typical adolescent development. Social media can support teens as they explore and discover more about themselves and their place in the grown-up world."

▶ **Place blame appropriately.** There are people online who do want to cause harm, and these individuals may unfortunately encourage your kids to do things you wish they wouldn't. While we can't protect kids from all online threats, we can help them look out for them. The AAP advice highlights that kids "may also not know about or choose not to use privacy settings, and they need to be warned that sex offenders often use social networking, chat rooms, email, and online gaming to contact and exploit children."

▶ **Expect mistakes.** Teens will inevitably make mistakes, but that is part of the learning process. The AAP recommends that parents "try to handle errors with empathy and turn a mistake into a teachable moment." That said, the AAP also encourages parents to look out for red flags (bullying, sexting, etc.) and to enlist professional help when needed.

The AAP screen time guidance encourages parents to exercise caution when giving kids access to social media, but what I really appreciated about their Family Media Use Plan is that it's not all doom and gloom. My take on the recommendations is that the doctors behind the guidance might be parents themselves. The guidance is well balanced, and it encourages parents to not see childhood access to screens and social media as an inherently bad thing.

## Key Takeaway: Kids Need Guidance *and* Autonomy

While we may want to control our children's every keystroke, it is important for parents to remember that kids do have an interest in privacy. Sometimes our desire to monitor their social media usage needs to be tempered. As my Dean, Laura Rosenbury, and her research partner, Professor Anne Dailey, illustrate in their article "The New Law of the Child," children "have interests in controlling the flow of information to their parents, especially when their actions and decisions may conflict with their parents' wishes."[128] As parents, one of our most important jobs is to help our children develop independence while also guiding them as they grow. Rosenbury and Dailey further explain, "More fully recognizing children's interests in personal integrity and privacy does not mean that all parental or state intrusions should be prohibited, but it will mandate different ways of balancing children's present and future interests against parental prerogatives."

Despite our best efforts, our kids aren't going to be perfect online. Their social media accounts will be overly disclosing, slightly embarrassing, and perhaps downright inappropriate at times. Hopefully, these mistakes will be sandwiched between positive online interactions that will nurture their transition to adulthood. Taking a misstep along the way is part of the learning process of growing up, and often, kids will learn, recalibrate, and grow as they move along the arch toward autonomy and independence. Parents, working in partnership with their growing kids, are key players in this process.

## CHAPTER ELEVEN

# Balance

I'd like to tell you I start most mornings with a moment of meditation as I sip tea watching the sun rise. But I don't.

Instead, most mornings, I scarf down a cup of hot coffee while scrolling my Facebook feed. I see what my friends have been up to. I'm impressed by how big their kids are getting, I check out Facebook memories, and I marvel at how much my own kids have changed.

Every few months, I take a Facebook hiatus, vowing to focus my time offline, but I keep going back. I love making new connections, and I love how social media fosters the friendships I have in real life.

But when I share on social media, I'm constantly reminded of the lessons I've learned over the past few years researching how we talk about kids online. The dangers of oversharing, the potential to violate my children's right to privacy, the importance of setting a good example online—all of these warnings flash in my head as I get ready to expand their digital footprints.

I asked members of one of my parenting Facebook groups if,

now that they've learned more about raising a family in a social media world, they tend to share more or less than they did when first getting social media accounts a little over a decade ago. Their varied responses suggest to me that the information we've gleaned over the past few years doesn't point to one clear answer.

**Question: Do you share more or less than you used to share? Why do you think your sharing habits have changed?**

- Less. The political climate has changed my sharing habits.

- About the same, but I am cautious about trying not to overrun my social media with baby posts because basically I used to hate when people did that!

- I definitely share less. I think I'm just overall too busy now for social media, so I mostly just share milestones in our life.

- Less. Acquired more "friends" I hadn't seen since high school and became more private/cautious as a result.

- Less. Opportunity to keep some details to close friends and protect family. Also time! Very busy with life.

- Less. Life has gotten busy, I've seen the effects of too much time on screens (for me personally), and I've realized that I spent too much time sharing and not enough time in the moment.

- I've never been a huge poster, so I don't know that I post less, but I am more aware of the things I post.

- Less, trying to be conscious of the online footprint I am creating for my children.

- I am more conscious about posting locations such as checking in at my daughter's school. Doing so seems like an added risk.

- Probably less. I'm too busy with work and two kids. I'll share photos through email with family who live far away.

- More because I have kids and Facebook is the way our out-of-town relatives keep up to date on them.

- I share more because of more extended/distant family involvement.

- I probably share more photos when I have newborns because I take more photos of them and spend more time sitting around on my phone nursing or rocking a baby. I haven't made a conscious effort to share more/less though.

- It varies. My husband is usually the sharer of kid pics and he is usually documenting a trip/adventure. I tend to share a lot when I have a newborn and less as they grow. I think I shared more when they were tiny, because I needed some form of "adult interaction" while alone with a newborn all day.

- More on Instagram. I show faraway shots where you can't zoom in to see my children's faces or shots of their hands, etc., I got more artsy with it.

- I think my sharing habits fluctuate. Some days, I publish three posts about my children. Sometimes I go two or three weeks without posting anything.

I loved reading these responses. As I collected them, I could imagine hearing my own voice come through each one. I'm not sure if I share more or less than I did a decade ago. But I know my access to social media, the amount of time I spend with a phone in hand, and the sheer number of post-worthy images I capture has certainly increased from my first days using social media through a BlackBerry device. It wasn't long ago that I saw my first iPhone, although now it is hard to imagine parenting without one.

## A Nuanced Approach

What has changed for me is that the conversations around sharing my story, and sharing my children's stories, have become more nuanced. Getting to know the families I met through my photography project constantly reminded me of the power of narratives. Working as a child abuse prosecutor reminded me of the dangers lurking past a parent's newsfeed. Becoming a mom to a growing teen reminded me that if I don't teach my children to exercise restraint online, they will have a harder time learning how to respect others' privacy in digital spaces.

I'm a work in progress when it comes to sharing online. I'm a wealth of knowledge but a constant contradiction. I share and delete; I embrace online communication and then shy away from it. But no matter how much I change my social media habits, my kids have already grown up shared. They've been shared in my newsfeed and in my parents' posts. They've had accounts on ClassDojo, and the youngest has been featured on the eldest's Instagram feed. Businesses have created ads with their images, and I've shared their names and interests with our local newspaper. They have digital footprints, and I hope that when they start walking across college campuses, they are OK with it.

Clearly, sharing our stories has many benefits. Sharing common parenting experiences brings communities together and helps connect similarly situated individuals around the globe.[129] As parents, we certainly *do* have an interest and right to freely express our life stories, and children are often central in that story's cast of characters. However, with each disclosure, a bit of our children's life story is no longer left for them to tell under their own terms. Equally important to the right of the child to one day narrate his or her own story is the child's right to never to share the information *at all*.

———

As I began studying the generation of kids growing up shared, I thought I'd find a simple legal solution that would help me understand how society could best balance a parent's right to share with a child's right to privacy. Since I was unable to do so, I turned to a different kind of solution. I looked to the research to figure out how we as a generation could continue to reap the benefits of online sharing while also protecting our kids online. I synthesized my research, and I've come up with a series of best practices to address the *perils* of growing up shared while still leaving its *power* to parents to harness. Over time, we are all beginning to recognize that there are inherent safety and moral risks involved in many of the ways we share online. But experts are also coming to some consensus about what we can do to share a bit more safely. These best practices, adopted from the literature and examined through a parenting lens of common sense, could be shared with parents, educators, pediatricians, policy-makers, and the media.[130] These best practices draw upon the wisdom of child psychologists and medical professionals, as well as research from top child safety advisors, those working in the field of child abductions and sexual abuse, and social media and internet experts.

These best practices were first published in my *Emory Law Journal* article "Sharenting: Children's Privacy in the Age of Social Media."[131] I also collaborated with my friend and colleague, Dr. Bahareh Keith, and we had the honor of presenting our recommendations at the annual conference of the American Academy of Pediatrics. We also adopted many of these best practices into our *JAMA Pediatrics* article "Parental Sharing on the Internet: Child Privacy in the Age of Social Media and the Pediatrician's Role."[132]

The proposed model reflects the importance of a parent's right to free expression but also encourages us to consider sharing only after weighing the potential harm of the information. Indeed, these best practices should not be seen as rules but as suggestions for parents inclined to use the internet in a way that will foster healthy child development.[133] We should consider the objects of our disclosure, our children, as autonomous persons entitled to protection not only from physical harm (such as the harm posed by pedophiles and identity thieves), but also from more intangible harms such as those that may come from inviting the world into our children's lives without first obtaining their permission to do so.

## BEST PRACTICES FOR SHARING ONLINE

### Familiarize Yourself with the Privacy Policies of the Sites on Which Kids Share

Many social sharing sites offer users the ability to select the specific audience for each photo or post shared.[134] Additionally, some sites give users the option of setting passwords and having their online content hidden from Google's search algorithm. Of course, we should always be cognizant of the inherent risks of website security breaches and the potential for a particular site to change or violate its policy without consent of the user. Understanding these policies is an important first step for families wanting to share with friends and family while limiting the future audience of their posts.

This isn't always easy, as privacy policies are not written in a way that consumers can easily understand. Therefore, we should encourage policy-makers to consider placing the burden on companies to provide information in plain language. Families are vulnerable consumers, and lawmakers should take steps to protect them through sound policy and regulation.[135] Corporations and marketers must take more proactive steps to protect children's privacy online—parents cannot do this alone.[136]

## Set Up Notifications to Alert You When Your Child's Name Appears in a Google Search Result

Once we decide to share information online, we will have an incredibly hard, if not impossible, time limiting the reach and life span of the information. However, in many cases, we can set up alerts to track where the information appears and monitor responses and third-party changes to their disclosures.[137] We can then evaluate the website and determine whether the shared content is appropriate.

## Consider Sharing Anonymously or in Private and Safe Facebook Groups

Some organizations host websites providing advice and support networks to parents struggling to solve their children's behavioral problems. These well-intentioned sites often invite us to share stories in the hopes of helping other parents. For example, a mother of a mentally ill child may be well intentioned when sharing her child's struggle, yet her online disclosures may reveal private information she didn't fully intend to share. While there are benefits to sharing this information, consider sharing and connecting without disclosing our full names or names of our children. If we decide to share our names, we should make sure we've fully thought through our choice and conclude that the benefits of sharing outweigh the risks to our child's long-term reputation.

## Use Caution When Sharing a Child's Actual Location

Many of us share our physical location online without thinking. Most social media apps do it automatically, and it can be tough to un-tag a location once it lands on our newsfeed. We sometimes are tagged by others at a specific location. We need to be mindful of this and avoid doing it too often, if at all. We need to remember that our intended audience, whether public or limited, might not always act with good intention. While child abductions and stalking that originate online are rare, the risk is heightened when personal information is shared.[138] Potential offenders not only have detailed information about a child's life, but also know the child's actual physical location and the family's routine. We should limit sharing our child's location in our posts and also consider shutting off our phones' GPS before sharing digital information on social media and blog sites, thus avoiding the inadvertent disclosures of such information.

## Let Kids Say No

By age four, children have developed at least some self-awareness.[139] At this young age, they are able to build friendships, have the ability to reason, and begin to compare themselves with others. If we *do* plan on posting on social media regularly, it would be a good practice to regularly talk about the internet with our kids. We can also seek out the right words to ask younger kids if they want their activities shared with friends and family. As is the case in many aspects of children's rights, the weight given to the child's choice should vary with respect to the age of the child and the information being disclosed. But parents should be mindful that even young children benefit from being heard and understood.

## Don't Share Pictures That Show Kids in Any State of Undress

I shared an adorable bottom picture of my third child as a newborn five years ago. I regret that now. I can safely say that in the almost nonexistent chance I have another baby, I, 100 percent, will not do that again. It was a terrible idea. While most view these images as cute and innocent, these images are easy targets for pedophiles and those wishing to profit from others seeking images of children.[140] Cybersafety expert Susan McLean states, "If you live your life vicariously through your kids online and you use photo-sharing sites and hashtags, you have to got to [sic] understand that that photo is worth something to someone else and it may not be for a purpose you like."

## Sharing's Effect on Well-Being

While most of the practices mentioned above are great ways to protect your child's footprint from *others*, this one really gets at protecting your kiddo's digital footprint from *you*.

First, we must consider that one day, our children will likely come face-to-face with our past online disclosures. Even when we limit the audience of posts, the full reach of the internet is far greater than many users consider. Deleted posts might have been saved before deletion. Moreover, "friends" today can later intentionally or inadvertently share information with the child or third parties even when the information was originally intended for a small audience. By being respectful about what we share about our kids online, we enhance the relationships we will have with them as they get older.

Second, we must consider the general effect that sharing has on a child's psychological development. Children model the behavior of their parents, and when we constantly share milestones, monitor social media accounts for likes and followers, and seek out recognition for what was once considered mundane daily life, children take note. One study found that by "enacting the value of fame, the majority of preadolescent participants use online video sharing sites (e.g., YouTube) to seek an audience beyond their immediate community."[141] Our children absorb messages from many sources, including the media and parents, and are likely to mimic observed behaviors in adolescence and adulthood. When our children see us sharing personal information in the public sphere, they will likely get the message that a public approach to sharing personal details about their lives is expected and appropriate.

## A Better Path Forward

These best practices shouldn't serve necessarily as rules, but as a guide as you further explore and embrace the culture shift that has taken place around modern family life. We've been focused on social media's role in how teens relate to one another and how technology has changed our work-life balance, but we've spent little time really exploring how social media and technology have redefined what growing up *looks* like and *feels* like. Our curated newsfeeds set a new reality for us as parents, and if we aren't careful, they will set a new, jaded reality for our children.

I want my five-year-old to meet people at a family reunion and tell them in person that she loves drawing and learning about dinosaurs, but in the meantime, I also want my cousins who are near and dear to my heart to get to know her despite our physical distance. When he asks, I want my eight-year-old to share his amazing gymnastics routine online, but I also want to do my best to ensure the videos don't get into a stranger's hands. I want my thirteen-year-old to learn and explore in his online world without my helicopter-like presence, but I struggle to resist the urge to protect him from social media's darkest spaces. Despite the knowledge I've accumulated over the years studying how social media affects our families, I've walked away from my research still wanting to share. Because somewhere entwined with my children's story is my own. Because despite its drawbacks, social media has added community and connections to our lives.

Through my work in this field, I've recognized that like so many other aspects of parenting, social media is a tool. Used appropriately, it helps us build relationships and connect with one another. But like any tool, we need to know its power before we pick it up. I set off on my research expecting to never want to share again, yet I came out of it with more questions than answers, and a strong sense that while there are perils of watching our children grow up on our social media feeds (and ultimately on their own feeds), there is also so much power in the practice of sharing our lives with our communities. Our job—as parents and child advocates—is to harness that power and look out for the perils so that our kids can benefit from the digital footprints left in childhood's wake.

# Acknowledgments

This book would not exist without the help, dedication, and support of so many. Thank you to my agent, Stacey Glick. When we first connected, you saw the book I would eventually write, even when I couldn't yet see it myself. Thank you for slowly pushing me to come out of my head and to open my heart.

Thank you, Anna Michels, for your steadfast support, your detailed editing, and most of all, your wisdom as my words took flight. I'm a novice author, and your patience and kindness meant the world to me. Thank you to Jenna Jankowski, Sharon Sofinski, Jessica Thelander, and Stephanie Washington for your detailed editing; Heather Morris, Jillian Rahn, and William T. Riley for their design work; Kay Birkner and Liz Kelsch for marketing and promotion; and the entire Sourcebooks team.

The idea for this book would not have grown past a short essay but for the tireless support I received from Dean Laura Rosenbury. Thank you, Laura, for pushing me past my comfort zone and supporting me every step of the way. Thank you to Lyrissa Lidsky, a friend and mentor who saw me through my imposter syndrome, always believing that my work was important and that my voice was strong. Thank you to Nancy Dowd for giving me the substance

I needed to become a children's rights scholar. Thank you, Amy Joyce, for taking a chance on me and giving me my first big break by accepting my essays for publication in the *Washington Post*. The seeds for this book were planted in those early essays. Thank you to Mari-Jane Williams, who continues to work with me at the *Post*, making my writing better with each edit.

There are so many colleagues at the University of Florida Levin College of Law who played an instrumental role in my scholarship. Thank you to the many members of our faculty who mentored me along the way to this book's publication. Thank you to my wonderful assistant, Coreen Yawn, and to Brittney Ladd, Megan Testerman, and all of my former research assistants who helped me develop the earlier ideas incorporated in this book.

Thank you to Judge Tim Browning, Judge Denise Ferrero, Brian Kramer, Ophir Lehavy, Judge James Nilon, Judge Meshon Rawls, Jeanne Singer, Magistrate Nancy Wilkov, and the many mentors who guided me throughout my career. There are so many of you who helped me grow as an attorney and, more importantly, as an empathetic human being. To my writing mentors, KJ Dell'Antonia, Devorah Heitner, Jess Lahey, Sue Scheff, and Allison Slater Tate. Thank you for giving of yourself even when I had nothing to offer.

The ideas in this book are not mine alone. Thank you to the many scholars who paved the way for me to do the deep thinking needed to put this work together. To Bahareh Keith, who sat alongside me propelling these ideas into the medical community. To the many parents who shared their stories with me, thank you for being vulnerable and honest. To Cole and to Sarah, but most of all, to Phoebe. Thank you for allowing me to bear witness to your pain, for allowing me to grow in your light.

Thank you to my students, my family, and my friends. Many of you read drafts of my work, shared my articles, gave me ideas, and rallied my spirits along the way as I wrote this book. You know who you are—I appreciate each one of you, and I am sorry I did not include all your names here. Special thanks to Mary Adkins, Anita and Gary Altschuler, Shana and Bob Amar, Nicole Bodlak, Kim Bosshardt, Tama Caldarone, Judy Clausen, Jonathan Cohen, Stephanie Comstock, Deborah Cupples, Jerry Deutsch, Teresa Drake, Andy Fass, Josh and Laura Gross, Jessica and Mike Gutter, Janna Harned, Adele Harris, Allison and Mike Haller, Amanda House, Kelly Imperi, Rabbi David Kaiman, Naava Katz, Stephanie Kirkconnell, Jill and Brian Koch, Holly and Ari Kurtz, Jennifer Kuvin, Lua Lepianka, Trisha Lolli, Judge Natalie Moore, Shalini Ray, Jennifer Sager, Josh Silverman, Danny Sokol, Holly Sprinkle, Amy Steinberg, Marcie Steinberg, Keri Wernecke, Mary K. Wimsett, Karen Yochim, Ronna Zaremski, and Jessica Zissimopulos for sharing your stories and allowing me to include references to some of them in this book.

Mom and Dad—thank you from here to eternity and back again. To my kiddos—being your mom makes me so proud. Thank you for giving me permission to share your stories in this book.

And to Ben—this book started with our conversations, it grew because of your support, and it will finally make its way into the world because you've stood anchored by my side. I love growing up sharing my life with you.

# Notes

1   Benjamin Shmueli and Ayelet Blecher-Prigat, "Privacy for Children,"
    *Columbia Human Rights Law Review* 42 (2010): 759.

2   I like to call this cohort of children coming of age under the watchful eyes
    of their parents' newsfeed "Generation Tagged," as first coined by James M.
    Oswald and Emma Nottingham in "The Not-So-Secret Life of Five-Year-
    Olds: Legal and Ethical Issues Relating to Disclosure of Information and the
    Depiction of Children on Broadcast and Social Media, *Journal of Media Law*,
    8, no. 2 (2016): 198–228. Two additional scholars who have explored paren-
    tal online sharing so well (and before I even began my work in the field)
    are Priya Kumar and Sarita Schoenebeck. In their article "The Modern
    Day Baby Book: Enacting Good Mothering and Stewarding Privacy on
    Facebook," the researchers interviewed mothers who use Facebook. The
    first line of this book borrows (with permission) a portion of their inter-
    view with one mother, identified in the article as "Marina." Kumar and
    Schoenebeck also introduce the concept of "privacy stewardship," which
    the authors describe as "the responsibility parents take on when deciding
    what is appropriate to share about their children online and ensuring that
    family and friends respect and maintain the integrity of those rules." Priya
    Kumar and Sarita Schoenebeck, "The Modern Day Baby Book: Enacting

Good Mothering and Stewarding Privacy on Facebook," *Proceedings of the 18th ACM Conference on Computer Supported Cooperative Work & Social Computing*, ACM, 2015.

3    For an excellent overview of how the landscape for children coming of age has changed in the past two decades, see John G. Palfrey and Urs Gasser, *Born Digital: Understanding the First Generation of Digital Natives* (New York: Basic Books, 2008).

4    Health Insurance Portability and Accountability Act, Pub. L. No. 104–191, 110 Stat. 1938 (1996) (codified as amended in scattered sections of 18 U.S.C., 26 U.S.C., 29 U.S.C., and 42 U.S.C.).

5    Family Educational Rights and Privacy Act, 20 U.S.C. § 1232g (2012).

6    "Safeguarding the Confidentiality of Youth in the Justice System: Recommendations and Resources," National Juvenile Justice Network, http://www.njjn.org/our-work/confidentiality-of-youth-in-justice-system -safeguards. ("[C]onfidentiality of court proceedings is necessary in order to safeguard a youth's privacy and protect them from the stigma and collateral consequences of juvenile justice involvement.")

7    Anne C. Dailey and Laura A. Rosenbury, "The New Law of the Child," *Yale Law Journal* 127 (2017): 1458.

8    Dailey and Rosenbury, "The New Law of the Child," 1459; citing Pierce v. Soc'y of Sisters, 268 U.S. 510, 534–35 (1925); see also Troxel v. Granville, 530 U.S. 57, 65 (2000).

9    See, e.g., David D. Meyer, "The Modest Promise of Children's Relationship Rights," *William and Mary Bill of Rights Journal* 11, no. 3 (2003): 1117, 1118. ("[C]ourts have not categorically rejected children's privacy rights, but have proceeded haltingly.")

10    Shmueli and Blecher-Prigat, "Privacy for Children," 759.

11    United Nations Convention on the Rights of the Child, https://www.unicef .org.uk/what-we-do/un-convention-child-rights/.

12   "UN Lauds Somalia as Country Ratifies Landmark Children's Rights Treaty," *UN News*, January 20, 2015, https://news.un.org/en/story/2015/01/488 692-un-lauds-somalia-country-ratifies-landmark-childrens-rights-treaty. South Sudan also signed the Convention later in 2015. "UN Lauds South Sudan as Country Ratifies Landmark Child Rights Treaty, *UN News*, May 4, 2015, https://news.un.org/en/story/2015/05/497732.

13   UNICEF United Kingdom, *The Rights of Every Child*, PDF available at https://www.unicef.org.uk/child-rights-partners/wp-content/uploads/sites /3/2016/08/CRC_summary_leaflet_Child_Rights_Partners_web_final.pdf.

14   Names of parents and children referenced throughout this book have been changed to protect their privacy.

15   Steven Leckart, "The Facebook-Free Baby," *Wall Street Journal*, May 12, 2012, https://www.wsj.com/articles/SB10001424052702304451104577392 041180138910.

16   *Collins English Dictionary*, s.v. "sharenting," https://www.collinsdictionary. com/dictionary/english/sharenting; Anita Singh, "New Scrabble Words: Genderqueer, Hackerazzo and Sharenting Added to Dictionary," *Telegraph*, May 2, 2019, https://www.telegraph.co.uk/news/2019/05/02/new-scrabble -words-genderqueer-hackerazzo-sharenting-added-dictionary/.

17   Maeve Duggan et al., "Parents and Social Media: Main Findings," Pew Research Center: Internet & Technology, July 16, 2015, https://www.pew internet.org/2015/07/16/main-findings-14/.

18   Duggan et al., "Parents and Social Media."

19   Deborah Lupton, "'It Just Gives Me a Bit of Peace of Mind': Australian Women's Use of Digital Media for Pregnancy and Early Motherhood," *Societies* 7, no. 3 (2017): 25. ("The research questions around which both the survey and focus groups were framed were: How are women using digital media for both pregnancy and parenting? Which digital media do they find most useful and valuable, and why? What media would they like

to use that are not currently available to them? What concerns (if any) do women have about the privacy and security of their personal data?"). For additional background on how parents share, see also Tawfiq Ammari, et al., "Managing Children's Online Identities: How Parents Decide What to Disclose About Their Children Online," *Proceedings of the 33rd Annual ACM Conference on Human Factors in Computing Systems*, ACM, April 2015: 1895–1904.

20    Maja Sonne Damkjær, "Sharenting = Good Parenting? Four Parental Approaches to Sharenting on Facebook," in *Digital Parenting*, eds. Giovanna Mascheroni, Cristina Ponte, and Ana Jorge (Gothenberg, Sweden: Nordicom, 2018). (Damkjær argues in her chapter that "to grasp the growing significance of sharenting, we must acknowledge that parents' approaches to communication technologies do not spring from rational, intentional decision making, but rather from the competing demands of social, work and family life, self-realisation and the desire to be good parents.")

21    Carrie Kerpen, "Stop Comparing Your Behind-the-Scenes with Everyone's Highlight Reel," *Forbes*, July 31, 2017, https://www.forbes.com/sites/carrie kerpen/2017/07/29/stop-comparing-your-behind-the-scenes-with-every ones-highlight-reel/#589bf23a073e. See also Brené Brown, *Daring Greatly: How the Courage to Be Vulnerable Transforms the Way We Live, Love, Parent, and Lead* (New York: Penguin, 2015).

22    Thank you to the parents in one of my favorite parenting Facebook groups who voluntarily agreed to anonymously answer some questions I posed about sharing on social media. Of course, this is a self-selected group of parents and is in no way intended to be considered scientific by any means. I viewed the feedback as conversational in nature, and the parents who answered my questions agreed to do so without attribution, knowing I would be writing a book.

23    Anna Brosch, "When the Child Is Born into the Internet: Sharenting as a

Growing Trend among Parents on Facebook," *The New Educational Review* 43, no. 1 (March 2016): 225–235. ("There is no doubt that Facebook offers today's parents a unique opportunity to exchange experiences and happiness about their parenthood or search for help with parenting issues. But the problems arise when they share embarrassing or too personal information about their children and therefore run a risk of breaching children's privacy.")

24    Alicia Blum-Ross and Sonia Livingstone, "Sharenting: Parent Blogging and the Boundaries of the Digital Self," *Popular Communication* 15, no. 2 (2017): 110–125.

25    For this phrase, Blum-Ross and Livingstone cite Katie Davis, "Tensions of Identity in a Networked Era: Young People's Perspectives on the Risks and Rewards of Online Self-Expression," *New Media & Society*, no. 4 (2012): 634–651.

26    C.S. Mott Children's Hospital, Mott Poll Report, *Parents on Social Media: Likes and Dislikes of Sharing*, March 16, 2015, mottpoll.org/reports-surveys /parents-social-media-likes-and-dislikes-sharenting. ("Parents rate social media as useful for making them feel like they are not alone (72%), learning what not to do (70%), getting advice from more experienced parents (67%), and helping them worry less (62%). In contrast, about two-thirds of parents are concerned about someone finding out private information about their child (68%) or sharing photos of their child (67%), while 52% are concerned that when older, their child might be embarrassed about what they have shared on social media... The majority of parents who use social media (74%) know of another parent who has shared too much information about a child on social media, including parents who gave embarrassing information about a child (56%), offered personal information that could identify a child's location (51%), or shared inappropriate photos of a child (27%).")

27    Material from my prior work in the *Emory Law Journal*, the *Kentucky Law*

*Journal,* and the *Washington Post* is included within this book, all with permission from the respective publishers. This passage contains some of the prior work.

28    Bree Holtz, Andrew Smock, and David Reyes-Gastelum, "Connected Motherhood: Social Support for Moms and Moms-to-Be on Facebook," *Telemedicine and e-Health* 21, no. 5 (2015): 415–421, citing J. B. Kane and C. Margerison-Zilko, "Theoretical Insights into Preconception Social Conditions and Perinatal Health: The Role of Place and Social Relationships," *Population Research and Policy Review* 36, no. 5 (2017): 639–669.

29    Stacey Steinberg, "#Advocacy: Social Media Activism's Power to Transform Law," *Kentucky Law Journal,* 105 (2016): 413.

30    Amy X. Zhang and Scott Counts, "Modeling Ideology and Predicting Policy Change with Social Media: Case of Same-Sex Marriage," *Proceedings of the 33rd Annual ACM Conference on Human Factors in Computing Systems,* ACM, April 2015: 2603–2612.

31    Munmun De Choudhury, Scott Counts, and Eric Horvitz, "Predicting Postpartum Changes in Emotion and Behavior via Social Media," *Proceedings of the SIGCHI Conference on Human Factors in Computing Systems,* ACM, 2013.

32    De Choudhury, Counts, and Horvitz, "Predicting Postpartum Changes." ("Nevertheless, we note that this type of research, and also results on the kinds of inferences that can be made from publicly available data pose interesting questions for individuals and for society more broadly. We have demonstrated that it is possible to make inferences from publicly available feeds about future psychological states that people may not wish to share with others. The predictions we make are similar to predictions about people made by systems in common use, including recommender systems that make inferences, e.g., about the titles of books that online users may wish to purchase given their history of purchases, search engines which guess

the intentions of people performing online searches, given past behavior and terms input in online searches, and predictions made by online services about the likelihood that a user will click on a particular advertisement.")

33   See Douglas NeJaime, "The Legal Mobilization Dilemma," *Emory Law Journal* 61 (2011).

34   See Darren L. Hutchinson, "Sexual Politics and Social Change," *Connecticut Law Review* 41 (2008).

35   The phrase "incidental advocacy" appears in L. Blackwell et al., "LGBT Parents and Social Media: Advocacy, Privacy, and Disclosure During Shifting Social Movements," *Proceedings of the 2016 CHI Conference on Human Factors in Computing Systems*, ACM, May 2016: 610–622.

36   L. Blackwell et al. "LGBT Parents and Social Media," 610–622. ("LGBT parents employ a number of complex strategies to navigate their public and private lives, managing the privacy of their children, partners, former partners and families in addition to their own. A significant body of research has shown that LGBT individuals use social media sites to address challenges they may face in their daily lives, such as social isolation and difficulty locating partners" (citations omitted).)

37   "Our Sharing Is Not Shaming," From the Bowels of Motherhood, July 29, 2015, http://fromthebowelsofmotherhood.blogspot.com/2015/07/our-sharing-is -not-shaming.html.

38   "Parenting in the Information Age: Am I Oversharing," Confessions of the Chromosomally Enhanced, August 13, 2015, http://www.confessions ofthechromosomallyenhanced.com/2015/08/parenting-in-information-age -am-i.html; Mary Farmer, "Our Sharing Is Not Shaming," From the Bowels of Motherhood, July 29, 2015, http://fromthebowelsofmotherhood.blog spot.com/2015/07/our-sharing-is-not-shaming.html.

39   Gabrielle Berman and Kerry Albright, "Children and the Data Cycle: Rights and Ethics in a Big Data World," *Innocenti Working Papers no.*

*2017–05*, UNICEF Office of Research—Innocenti, Florence, 2017. https://www.unicef-irc.org/publications/pdf/IWP_2017_05.pdf.

40    Allen St. John, "Amazon Echo Dot Kids Violates Privacy Rules, Advocates Claim," *Consumer Reports*, May 9, 2019, https://www.consumerreports.org/privacy/amazon-echo-dot-kids-violates-privacy-rules-advocates-claim/. I declined to give an interview on the topic, as this issue was brand new to me at the time the article was initially reported. Mr. John is an excellent reporter, and I've learned a lot about privacy and technology through his meticulous work.

41    Matt O'Brien, "Parents Can't Delete What Kids Tell Amazon Voice Assistant." AP News, May 9, 2019, https://www.apnews.com/f062c28ae72 144b3b22146d9d4c6fab3. The article also cited to a *Consumer Reports* article. ("Consumer Reports said that its own tests also found that the Echo Dot Kids remembered information that was deleted, including a birth date and the color of a dog. The nonprofit organization said its researchers were able to delete data from regular versions of Echo Dot and Alexa.")

42    Dictionary.com, s.v. "dark web," https://www.dictionary.com/browse/dark -web?s=t.

43    Google, "Find Related Images with Reverse Image Search," https://support .google.com/websearch/answer/1325808?co=GENIE.Platform%3DAndroid &hl=en.

44    Jennifer O'Neill, "The Disturbing Facebook Trend of Stolen Kid Photos," Yahoo! Parenting, March 3, 2015, https://www.yahoo.com/parenting/mom -my-son-was-digitally-kidnapped-what-112545291567.html. ("Lindsey Paris was excited when she saw a new 'like' pop up on the Facebook page that she'd set up for her blog Red Head Baby Mama. But the feeling quickly turned into shock after the Atlanta mother clicked on the name of the woman who'd given the thumbs up to a photo of Paris's then 18-month-old son. The stranger had made the toddler's image her homepage photo and

was presenting Paris's son as her own child. 'I flew into a mother lion rage, then I burst into tears,' Paris tells Yahoo Parenting of the 2012 incident that still has her on edge. 'She was pretending that he was her own and commenting on when was he going to start teething. Her friends were saying that they loved his hair. She was treating him as her own and that was the most petrifying thing. I didn't know people did this.'")

45   Scott Stump, "Who's Following You? Mom Finds Son's Photo on Creepy Instagram Page," *Today*, August 15, 2019, https://www.today.com/parents /mom-finds-son-s-photo-social-media-photos-kids-t160770.

46   "Digital Birth: Welcome to the Online World," Business Wire, October 6, 2010,   https://www.businesswire.com/news/home/20101006006722/en /Digital-Birth-Online-World.

47   Tehila Minkus, Kelvin Liu, and Keith W. Ross, "Children Seen but Not Heard: When Parents Compromise Children's Online Privacy," *Proceedings of the 24th International Conference on the World Wide Web*, WWW15 (2015), http://cse.poly.edu/~tehila/pubs/WWW2015children.pdf.

48   Alexa K. Fox and Mariea Grubbs Hoy, "Smart Devices, Smart Decisions? Implications of Parents' Sharenting for Children's Online Privacy: An Investigation of Mothers," *Journal of Public Policy & Marketing* 38.4 (2019): 414–432. While this study focused on mothers, the researchers intend to also speak with fathers in future work. ("Future research is needed to explore how new fathers, single parents, and grandparents may experience vulnerability and how it relates to protecting children's online privacy.")

49   Fox and Grubbs Hoy, "Smart Devices, Smart Decisions?" ("Companies must understand how marketing is contributing to societal pressure to be a 'good parent,' and they must find ways to help parents as they navigate to new stages of life. Brands, social networks, and advocacy organizations can play a key role in helping mothers understand the safety implications of their social media behaviors by highlighting the privacy issues related to

posting information about their children on social media instead of encouraging them to engage in such activity.")

50　Sharon Kirkey, "Do You Know Where Your Child's Image Is? Pedophiles Sharing Photos from Parents' Social Media Accounts," *National Post* 18, April 2017, http://nationalpost.com/news/canada/photos-shared-on-pedophile-sites-taken-from-parents-social-media-accounts.

51　Canadian Centre for Child Protection, https://www.cybertip.ca/app/en/. (One of the tipline's mandates is to protect the public by "[r]eceiving and processing tips...about potentially illegal material, as well as activities regarding the online sexual exploitation of children, and referring any relevant leads to the appropriate law enforcement agency and/or child welfare agency...")

52　Lucy Battersby, "Millions of Social Media Photos Found on Child Exploitation Sharing Sites," *Sydney Morning Herald*, September 30, 2015, http://www.smh.com.au/national/millions-of-social-media-photos-found-on-child-exploitation-sharing-sites-20150929-gjxe55.html.

53　See, e.g., United States v. Hotaling, 634 F.3d 725, 727 (2d Cir. 2011) (describing how one defendant created morphed images). See also: Stacey Steinberg, "Changing Faces: Morphed Child Pornography and the First Amendment." *Emory Law Journal* (2019): 19–24.

54　See generally New York v. Ferber, 458 U.S. 747, 764 (1982) (holding child pornography is not in the realm of First Amendment protection).

55　See, e.g., United States v. Hotaling, 634 F.3d 725, 727 (2d Cir. 2011) (describing how one defendant created morphed images).

56　Ashcroft v. Free Speech Coal., 535 U.S. 234, 241 (2002).

57　Prosecutorial Remedies and Other Tools to End the Exploitation of Children Today (PROTECT) Act of 2003, Pub. L. No. 108–21, 117 Stat. 650 (codified as amended in scattered sections of 18 U.S.C. and 34 U.S.C.).

58　For a more nuanced discussion of this issue, see Ian C. Ballon, *E-Commerce and Internet Law: Treatise with Forms* (Eagan, MN: West, 2009): Section 40.01[2]. ("Unlike computer-created images or depictions of adults altered to appear to be child pornography, at least one court has held that a morphed depiction of actual children (in this case, an identifiable child's face superimposed on the body of a young naked boy in a suggestive pose) was not protected by the First Amendment and could serve as the basis for a child pornography possession conviction under the CPPA.") (citing United States v. Bach, 400 F.3d 622 (8th Cir.), *cert. denied*, 546 U.S. 901 (2005)).

59    Parker v. State, 81 So. 3d 451, 453 (Fla. Dist. Ct. App. 2011) (holding that Florida's child pornography statute does not criminalize morphed child pornography because the sexual conduct depicted must be of children).

60    Marion Oswald, Helen James, and Emma Nottingham, "The Not-So-Secret Life of Five-Year-Olds: Legal and Ethical Issues Relating to Disclosure of Information and the Depiction of Children on Broadcast and Social Media." *Journal of Media Law* 8, no. 2 (2016): 198–228.

61    The idea of a child native to digital spaces appears in a 1996 paper: John Perry Barlow, "A Declaration of the Independence of Cyberspace," Electronic Frontier Foundation, February 8, 1996, https://www.eff.org/cyberspace-independence. ("You are terrified of your own children, since they are natives in a world where you will always be immigrants. Because you fear them, you entrust your bureaucracies with the parental responsibilities you are too cowardly to confront yourselves. In our world, all the sentiments and expressions of humanity, from the debasing to the angelic, are parts of a seamless whole, the global conversation of bits. We cannot separate the air that chokes from the air upon which wings beat.")

I am more familiar with the term as used by Dr. Devorah Heitner, PhD, one of the leading experts on this subject. Her website, https://www.raising digitalnatives.com/, is full of advocacy and advice for families in the digital age.

62    ComRes, "Safer Internet Day 2017," February 2017, https://www.comres global.com/wp-content/uploads/2017/02/BBC-Safer-Internet-Day-2017 _Data-Tables_Updated-25th-Jan.pdf.

63    Alexis Hiniker, Sarita Y. Schoenebeck, and Julie A. Kientz, "Not at the Dinner Table: Parents' and Children's Perspectives on Family Technology Rules." *Proceedings of the 19th ACM Conference on Computer-Supported Cooperative Work & Social Computing*, ACM, 2016.

64    Carol Moser, Tianying Chen, and Sarita Y. Schoenebeck, "Parents' and Children's Preferences about Parents Sharing about Children on Social Media," *Proceedings of the 2017 CHI Conference on Human Factors in Computing Systems*, ACM, 2017.

65    Moser, Chen, and Schoenebeck, "Parents' and Children's Preferences."

66    Cole Delbyck, "Gwyneth Paltrow Gets Called Out by Daughter Apple for Nonconsensual Selfie," *Huffington Post*, March 26, 2019, https://www.huffpost .com/entry/gwyneth-paltrow-daughter-nonconsensual-selfie_n_5c9a2fab e4b0d42ce360f91b.

67    Kate Lyons, "Apple Martin Tells Off Mother Gwyneth Paltrow for Sharing Photo Without Consent," *Guardian*, March 26, 2016, https://www.the guardian.com/film/2019/mar/29/apple-martin-tells-mother-gwyneth -paltrow-off-for-sharing-photo-without-consent.

68    Phoebe Maltz Bovy, "The Ethical Implications of Parents Writing About Their Kids," *Atlantic*, January 15, 2013, http://www.theatlantic.com/sexes /archive/2013/01/the-ethical-implications-of-parents-writing-about-their -kids/267170/.

69    Maltz Bovy, "The Ethical Implications." She defines the concept this way: "Parental overshar[ing]...does not refer to parents discussing their kids with friends and family... Two criteria must be present: first, the children need to be identifiable. That does not necessarily mean full names. The author's full

name is plenty, even if the children have a different (i.e. their father's) last name. Next, there needs to be ambition to reach a mass audience."

70   Liza Long, "I Am Adam Lanza's Mother," *Blue Review*, December 15, 2013, https://thebluereview.org/i-am-adam-lanzas-mother/. See also Maltz Bovy, "The Ethical Implications." ("Online commenters and reviewers often ignore that parents may misjudge their own parenting. More upsettingly, they do not question the acceptability of parents mining kids' lives for material. Perhaps they assume these kids are if anything privileged to have such attentive (and often well-connected) parents.

Where, then, should a parent-writer draw the line? The simplest way is to ask if a given anecdote would be appropriate if its subject were not your child. Would you publish that essay about your colleague or sibling? About a friend's kid? If you consider the power dynamics between parent and child; the childhood secrets only a parent can know; and the trust children have in their parents, you see why parental overshare, however well-intentioned, is unethical.")

71   David Chazan, "French Parents 'Could Be Jailed' for Posting Children's Photos Online," *Telegraph*, March 1, 2016, https://www.telegraph.co.uk/news /worldnews/europe/france/12179584/French-parents-could-be-jailed-for -posting-childrens-photos-online.html.

72   Nicole Kobie, "Could Children One Day Sue Parents for Posting Baby Pics on Facebook?" *Guardian*, May 8, 2016, https://www.theguardian.com /sustainable-business/2016/may/08/children-sue-parents-facebook-post -baby-photos-privacy.

73   In her article "Hatching the Egg: A Child-Centered Perspective on Parent's Rights," Barbara Bennett Woodhouse critiques commonly held beliefs regarding the role of parents in the upbringing of children. She suggests that parents should act as stewards rather than as owners with respect to

their children. Barbara Bennett Woodhouse, "Hatching the Egg: A Child-Centered Perspective on Parent's Rights," 14 *Cardozo Law Review* 1747 (1993).

74    Devorah Heitner, *Screenwise: Helping Kids Thrive (and Survive) in Their Digital World* (Routledge, 2018).

75    Yalda T. Uhls and Patricia M. Greenfield, "The Value of Fame: Preadolescent Perceptions of Popular Media and Their Relationship to Future Aspirations," *Developmental Psychology* 48, no. 2 (2012): 315, http://www.ncbi.nlm.nih.gov/pubmed/2218229.

76    Julia Cho, "Is the Immediate Playback of Events Changing Children's Memories?" *New York Times*, April 25, 2019, https://www.nytimes.com/2019/04/25/well/family/video-altering-memory.html?module=inline.

77    Nadine Davidson-Wall, "'Mum, Seriously!' Sharenting the New Social Trend with No Opt-Out," paper presented at the 9th Debating Communities and Social Networks 2018 OUA Conference, online conference, 2018.

78    KJ Dell'Antonia, "Facebook Is Stealing Your Family's Joy," *New York Times*, April 12, 2019, https://www.nytimes.com/2019/04/12/opinion/sunday/facebook-privacy-parenting.html.

79    Allison Slater Tate, "Our Relatives Survived the Holocaust. How Do We Tell Kids about Charlottesville?" *Today*, August 17, 2017, https://www.today.com/parents/how-talk-kids-about-anti-semitism-america-t115227.

80    Jeffrey Shulman, "The Parent as (Mere) Educational Trustee: Whose Education Is It, Anyway," *Nebraska Law Review* 89 (2010): 290.

81    The authors (Berman and Albright) explain this a bit further by referencing additional research. The full citations are excluded here but can be found in the article (citation provided in endnote 39). "('One of the most critical issues as relates to Big Data and children is the impact on their digital identities over their life course.') As noted by Papacharissi (2010), '[the] networked self is an amalgam of identities that are created across multiple online

platforms, constituted via an array of social media tools." Helmond (2010) adds two concepts to this idea: first, that this identity online is in perpetual beta, implying that the nature of these software platforms results in the acquisition of information (updates, photographs, additional information) ad infinitum, leading to a constantly evolving representation of self. Second, that an individual's/child's material online is often generated by other users and the written and visual images provided may have greater impact on an individual's/child's networked self than that which they provided themselves."

82  1 Second Everyday, https://1se.co/.

83  Kate O'Flaherty, "Facebook Data Breach—What to Do Next." *Forbes*, September 29, 2018, https://www.forbes.com/sites/kateoflahertyuk/2018 /09/29/facebook-data-breach-what-to-do-next/#50e3faf22de3. ("Facebook notified users of a massive data breach affecting over 50 million people. The breach had taken place three days earlier, on the afternoon of 25 September.

The social media giant says it doesn't know exactly what kind of information has been compromised. However, in an updated statement yesterday, it did admit the hack affected those who use Facebook to log into other accounts... [Facebook] believes it has fixed the security vulnerability, which enabled hackers to exploit a weakness in Facebook's code to access the 'View As' privacy tool that allows users to see how their profile looks to other people.")

84  Mike Ribble, Gerald Bailey, and Tweed Ross, "Digital Citizenship: Addressing Appropriate Technology Behavior," *Learning & Leading with Technology* 32, no. 1 (2004): 6. (One of the study authors, Mike Ribble, runs a website, digitalcitizenship.net. On his website, he explains that "Digital Citizenship is a concept which helps teachers, technology leaders and parents to understand what students/children/technology users should know to use technology appropriately.")

85  Brigid Schulte, "Making Time for Kids? Study Says Quality Trumps

Quantity," *Washington Post*, March 28, 2015, https://www.washington post.com/local/making-time-for-kids-study-says-quality-trumps-quantity /2015/03/28/10813192-d378-11e4-8fce-3941fc548f1c_story.html?utm_term =.f91ff561a13a. ("In fact, the study found one key instance when parent time can be particularly harmful to children. That's when parents, mothers in particular, are stressed, sleep-deprived, guilty and anxious.

'Mothers' stress, especially when mothers are stressed because of the juggling with work and trying to find time with kids, that may actually be affecting their kids poorly,' said co-author Kei Nomaguchi, a sociologist at Bowling Green State University.

That's not to say that parent time isn't important. Plenty of studies have shown links between quality parent time—such as reading to a child, sharing meals, talking with them or otherwise engaging with them one-on-one— and positive outcomes for kids. The same is true for parents' warmth and sensitivity toward their children. It's just that the quantity of time doesn't appear to matter.")

86    Stacey Steinberg, "Parents' Social Media Habits Are Teaching Children the Wrong Lessons," *Washington Post*, https://www.washingtonpost.com /news/parenting/wp/2017/07/31/parents-social-media-habits-are-teaching -kids-the-wrong-lessons/.

87    Stacey Steinberg, "Sharenting: Children's Privacy in the Age of Social Media," 66 *Emory Law Journal*, no. 839 (2017).

88    The right to be forgotten arose in the "landmark ruling" of Google Spain SL v. Mario Consteja González. See Chelsea E. Carbone, "To Be or Not to Be Forgotten: Balancing the Right to Know with the Right to Privacy in the Digital Age," 22 *Virginia Journal of Social Policy and the Law* 525 (2015) (referring to this case as a "landmark ruling" and describing the implementation of the right to be forgotten following the decision).

89    Ioannis Iglezakis, "The Right to Be Forgotten in the Google Spain Case

(Case C-131/12): A Clear Victory for Data Protection or an Obstacle for the Internet?" July 26, 2014, https://ssrn.com/abstract-2472323.

90    Meyer v. Nebraska, 262 U.S. 390 (1923).

91    Pierce v. Society of Sisters, 268 U.S. 510 (1925).

92    Nguon v. Wolf, 517 F. Supp. 2d 1177, 1183, 1193–94 (C.D. Cal. 2007).

93    Sidis v. FR Publishing Corp. 113 F.2d 806 (2d Cir. 1940).

94    Amy Gajda, "Privacy, Press, and the Right to Be Forgotten in the United States," 93 *Washington Law Review* 201 (2018).

95    Senator Ed Markey and Senator Josh Hawley, Press Release, https://www .markey.senate.gov/news/press-releases/senators-markey-and-hawley -introduce-bipartisan-legislation-to-update-childrens-online-privacy-rules.

96    Allyson Haynes Stuart, "Google Search Results: Buried If Not Forgotten." *North Carolina Journal of Law and Technology* 15 (2013): 463. Stuart explains that in the United States, "any information posted online is considered speech," while in the European Union, "the online posting of information" is the processing of "'data' which is owned by the individual subject." Her argument does not address the posting of information by parents, but I found her work to be enlightening as I explored these issues.

97    Stacey Steinberg, "The Online Back to School Checklist Your Kids Need You to Have," *Washington Post*, September 9, 2019, https://www .washingtonpost.com/lifestyle/2019/09/09/online-privacy-checklist-your -kids-need-you-have/.

98    "Family Outraged after Video of Toddler Frightened by the Easter Bunny Goes Viral," CBS News, April 6, 2018, https://www.cbsnews.com/news /kissimmee-florirda-easter-bunny-family-outraged-after-video-of-frightened -2-year-old-goes-viral/.

99    National Conference of State Legislatures, "Privacy Protections in State Constitutions," November 7, 2018, http://www.ncsl.org/research /telecommunications-and-information-technology/privacy-protections

-in-state-constitutions.aspx. ("Constitutions in 11 states—Alaska, Arizona, California, Florida, Hawaii, Illinois, Louisiana, Montana, New Hampshire, South Carolina and Washington—have explicit provisions relating to a right to privacy. New Hampshire voters approved a new constitutional amendment in the Nov. 2018 election. The privacy protections afforded in some of these states mirror the Fourth Amendment of the U.S. Constitution relating to search and seizure or government surveillance, but add more specific references to privacy *[shown in italics]*. In addition, more general provisions in other states have been interpreted by courts to have established privacy rights or various types.")

100 Doug Linder, "The Right of Privacy: Is It Protected by the Constitution," http://law2.umkc.edu/faculty/projects/ftrials/conlaw/rightofprivacy.html.

101 Howell v. New York Post Co., 81 N.Y.2d 115, 123, 612 N.E.2d 699, 703 (1993).

102 Ronald Sullivan, "Steinberg is Guilty of First-Degree Manslaughter," *New York Times*, January 31, 1989, https://www.nytimes.com/1989/01/31/nyregion/steinberg-is-guilty-of-first-degree-manslaughter.html.

103 For a more detailed discussion of the major shifts taking place as big data becomes commonplace in educational settings, see Leah Plunkett and Urs Gasser, "Student Privacy and Ed Tech (K–12) Research Briefing," Berkman Center Research Publication No. 2016-15, September 26, 2016, https://papers.ssrn.com/sol3/papers.cfm?abstract_id=2842800. The authors explain, "Formal and informal connected learning environments are both strengthening and disrupting brick & mortar K-12 public school systems."

104 Deborah Lupton and Ben Williamson, "The Datafied Child: The Dataveillance of Children and Implications for Their Rights," *New Media & Society* 19.5 (2017): 780–794.

105 Emmie Saner, "ClassDojo: Do We Really Need an App That Could Make Classrooms Overly Competitive?" *Guardian*, April 30, 2018, https://www.theguardian.com/education/shortcuts/2018/apr/30/classdojo-do-we-really

-need-an-app that could-make-classrooms-overly-competitive. See also the homepage of ClassDojo, https://www.classdojo.com/.

106  Natasha Singer, "Privacy Concerns for ClassDojo and Other Tracking Apps for Schoolchildren." *New York Times*, November 16, 2014, https://www .nytimes.com/2014/11/17/technology/privacy-concerns-for-classdojo-and -other-tracking-apps-for-schoolchildren.html.

107  Benjamin Herold, "Maryland Dad Wants June 30 to Be 'National Student Data Deletion Day,'" July 7, 2017, Education Week, http://blogs.edweek.org /edweek/DigitalEducation/2017/06/dad_wants_june_30_student_data _deletion_day.html.

108  Brad Shear, "June 30th: National Student Data Deletion Day For K–12 Public Schools," Shear on Social Media, Law, Life & Tech, June 26, 2017, https://www.shearsocialmedia.com/2017/06/june-30th-national-student -data-deletion-day-k-12-schools.html.

109  Sue Scheff, Melissa Schorr, and Monica S. Lewinsky, *Shame Nation: The Global Epidemic of Online Hate* (Naperville, IL: Sourcebooks, 2018).

110  Aurora Szentágotai-Tătar, et al., "Shame and Guilt-Proneness in Adolescents: Gene-Environment Interactions," *PLOS ONE* 10.7 (2015): e0134716. See also Brené Brown, *Daring Greatly*.

111  Shmueli and Blecher-Prigat, "Privacy for Children," 759.

112  Anya Kamenetz, *The Art of Screen Time: How Your Family Can Balance Digital Media and Real Life*, (New York: PublicAffairs, 2018).

113  Kamenetz, *The Art of Screen Time*.

114  Sonia Livingstone and Jasmina Byrne, "Parenting in the Digital Age: The Challenges of Parental Responsibility in Comparative Perspective," https:// www.nordicom.gu.se/sv/system/tdf/kapitel-pdf/01_livingstone_byrne .pdf?file=1&type=node&id=39888&force=. ("It seems that the old saying "it takes a village to raise a child" still applies in a digital world. It's just that the village is now both local and Global.")

115  Somini Sengupta, "Sharing, with a Safety Net," *New York Times*, September 19, 2013, http://www.nytimes.com/2013/09/20/technology/bill-provides -reset-button-for-youngsters-online-posts.html.

116  Sengupta, "Sharing, with a Safety Net." "It was the first state to require companies to report data breaches, and it requires Web sites and mobile apps to post privacy policies that explain how personal information is used. A recently passed law requires Web sites to tell users whether they honor browsers' do-not-track signals."

117  Milovan Savic and Kath Albury, "Most Adults Have Never Heard of TikTok—That's by Design," Inverse, July 18, 2019, https://www.inverse.com /article/57815-what-is-tiktok-why-most-know-nothing-about-it.

118  Chavie Lieber, "TikTok Is the Latest Social Media Platform Accused of Abusing Children's Privacy—Now It's Paying Up," Vox, February 28, 2019, https://www.vox.com/the-goods/2019/2/28/18244996/tiktok-children -privacy-data-ftc-settlement.

119  Shelby Brown, "TikTok, Livestreaming Apps Are 'Hunting Ground' for Abusers, Warn Kids' Advocates," CNET, February 25, 2019, https://www .cnet.com/news/tiktok-live-streaming-apps-are-hunting-ground-for -abusers-warn-childrens-advocates/.

120  Support Center, TikTok, https://support.tiktok.com/en/privacy-safety /for-parents-default.

121  Caitlin Costello, D. E. McNeil, and R. L. Binder, "Adolescents and Social Media: Privacy, Brain Development, and the Law," *Journal of the American Academy of Psychiatry and the Law* 44.3 (2016): 313–21.

122  Wait until 8th, https://www.waituntil8th.org/. (According to the website, "The Wait Until 8th pledge empowers parents to rally together to delay giving children a smartphone until at least 8th grade.")

123  PBS, "Social and Emotional Development," last visited January 22, 2017, http://www.pbs.org/wholechild/abc/social.html.

124  Bark, "How It Works." https://www.bark.us/#how.

125  Our Pact, "Premium Features," https://ourpact.com/.

126  "Family Media Use Plan," American Academy of Pediatrics, HealthyChildren .org, https://www.healthychildren.org/English/media/Pages/default.aspx.

127  "Family Media Use Plan."

128  Dailey and Rosenbury, "The New Law of the Child," 1503.

129  Nina Criscuolo, "'Sharenting' Offers Benefits for Parents, Safety Concerns for Children," WISHTV, May 11, 2015, http://wishtv.com/2015/05/06 /sharenting-offers-benefits-for-parents-safety-concerns-for-children/.

130  See generally Gwenn Schurgin O'Keeffe, Kathleen Clarke-Pearson, and Council on Communications and Media, "Clinical Report—The Impact of Social Media on Children, Adolescents, and Families," Pediatrics 127, no. 4 (April 2011): 800–804, http://pediatrics.aappublications.org/content /127/4/800 (noting that in similar contexts, pediatricians are in a unique position to help parents and children safely navigate the internet).

131  Steinberg, "Sharenting: Children's Privacy."

132  Bahareh E. Keith and Stacey Steinberg, "Parental Sharing on the Internet: Child Privacy in the Age of Social Media and the Pediatrician's Role," JAMA Pediatrics 171, no. 5 (May 1, 2017): 413–414. https://www.ncbi.nlm.nih.gov /pubmed/28346593.

133  John Stewart, "Ethics and Social Media: Responses to Panetta, Schlimm, and Supple Bartels," Character and...Soc. Media 1, no. 71 (2015): 72–73.

134  Jimit Bagadiya, "The Ultimate Guide on How to Manage Social Media Privacy Settings," Social Pilot, last visited January 22, 2017, https://socialpilot.co/blog /ultimate-guide-manage-social-media-privacy-settings/ (providing instruc- tions for how to manage privacy settings on Facebook, Twitter, Pinterest, LinkedIn, and Instagram to restrict viewership to intended audiences).

135  My colleague, Professor Catalina Goanta of Maastricht University in the Netherlands, shared with me a website called pribot.org, which helps

consumers understand the privacy policies of the websites with which they interact.

136  This idea crystalized for me during the 2019 "Digital Lives" Conference at the Swiss Institute of Comparative Law, thanks to discussions with Professor Urs Gasser, Executive Director of the Berkman Klein Center for Internet and Society at Harvard University.

137  Nione Meakin, "The Pros and Cons of 'Sharenting,'" *Guardian*, May 18, 2013, http://www.theguardian.com/lifeandstyle/2013/may/18/pros-cons-of -sharenting (providing instructions for setting up a Google alert).

138  "Teen Internet Statistics," Online Safety Site, January 22, 2017, http://www .onlinesafetysite.com/PI/Teenstats.htm (reporting results of a study that demonstrated the relative rarity of child abductions and stalking).

139  PBS, "Social and Emotional Development." You can learn more about the ages and stages of child development at this website.

140  Battersby, "Millions of Social Media Photos Found." ("Senior investigator at the eSafety Commissioner, Toby Dagg, said that on one site with at least 45 million images 'about half the material appeared to be sourced directly from social media' and clearly labelled in folders as images from Facebook, or other social sites like Kik, with one folder called 'Kik girls'. Another was labelled 'My daughter's Instagram friends'.

While photos copied from social media would not be considered exploitation material on their own, they were often accompanied by comments that explicitly sexualise the children. However, this was just a fraction of all the material investigated every year, Mr Dagg added.")

141  Uhls and Greenfield, "The Value of Fame."

# Index

# About the Author

Stacey Steinberg is a legal skills professor at the University of Florida Levin College of Law, where she supervises the Gator TeamChild Juvenile Law Clinic. She is an internationally sought-after expert on children's privacy. Her article "Sharenting: Children's Privacy in the Age of Social Media" was the first scholarly legal paper focused at the intersection of a parent's right to share and a child's interest in privacy. Steinberg's work has been cited by news and research organizations including NPR, the *New York Times*, the *Washington Post*, CNN, and the children's rights arm of the United Nations, UNICEF. She contributes to On Parenting from the *Washington Post* and is a self-taught photographer. Steinberg previously worked as a special victims unit prosecutor and as a children's legal services attorney. She lives with her husband and three kids in Florida, where she continues to share (with her children's permission) on social media.